MARVEL

SPIDER-MAN
Miles Morales
GUIDE

TABLE OF CONTENTS

Walkthrough

Mission 1: Hold Onto Your Web-Shooters

Location: Harlem

Rewards: 3,500 XP

Meet Pete at Midtown

On your way from the Bronx down to Midtown, be sure to get back in the swing of things, so to speak. Familiarize the means of traversal, using swinging, wall-running, web zipping and zipping to points. Good traversal is just as important as combat, so practice moving low to the ground, going high, and boosting when no big buildings are in sight.

When you're ready to move things along, head up to the missing site to meet with Peter Parker.

Defeat the Prisoners

When things inevitably go wrong as they always do, Peter will leave Miles with the task of containing the escaping prisoners all by himself. Not to worry, as Miles is more than capable even as a rookie Spider-Man.

While Miles has many of the moves Peter does, he's pretty fast - but might not be as strong yet. The most important thing in these first fights is to avoid taking blows or getting overwhelmed. Always be on the lookout to dodge incoming attacks or gunfire, and get around behind your opponents. You'll also have your web shooter gadget, to launch up to six shots at a time while they slowly regenerate back. Three shots can web up an enemy to stun them, and knocking them against the wall or floor will make them stick for good.

When more prisoners enter the fray, they'll start to employ weapons. Shutting down ranged attackers will be a top priority - so remember to use your webs to take the guns right out of their hands, or use anything lying around to throw at and stun them. Others may run to pick up the weapons, so use that time to beat them down while they're distracted.

Catch Rhino

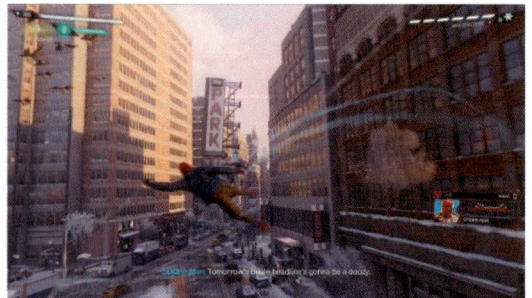

As Peter and his adversary move off deeper into downtown, try your best to keep up with them by swinging and zipping to maintain your top speed at all times.

Be ready for when you see Rhino leap up to the side of a building - he'll toss parking signs your way that you'll need to dodge in midair or risk taking damage and slowing you down.

Once you get a hold of Rhino yourself, you'll need to reign in the unstoppable charger by moving him side to side. This won't slow him down, but avoiding cars, signs, and other obstacles will help you avoid damage - and that's something you don't want to have to worry about right now.

Don't worry about innocent bystanders, Peter will run interference to keep them out of harm's way - though you'll be able to do a bit of hero work yourself by looking for the right button prompts. Mostly, you're going to want to look ahead to spot the brightly colored mall directory ads and steer around them.

When you get back outside, don't worry about following him into the side of a building - he'll pop out around the corner, so just worry about keeping close while he takes the high road and dodge any more parking signs coming your way until you reach the Roxxon Plant.

Defeat the Prisoners (Again)

Once again you'll have to deal with a group of prisoners - now armed with bigger weaponry including a rocket launcher. Dodge to the side and move in close to get behind and take them out, and try holding down the attack button to launch enemies into the air, and use aerial attacks to stay out of range of the others.

When the first group of prisoners go down, look to the nearby rooftops for more prisoners firing from above. Zip up to the railing and dive in to attack, and then disable the gunners with your webbing, or throw nearby debris at them.

You'll need to keep advancing between rooftops to take out more prisoners, so keep an eye on incoming fire signs to know where the next group of enemies is trying to shoot you from. At this point, you'll be able to rack up enough combo points to start performing instant takedowns - which are great for taking out a troublesome sniper before they can make use of their weapon.

When the last group on the bridge goes down, head to the next marker to find Pete.

Defeat Rhino

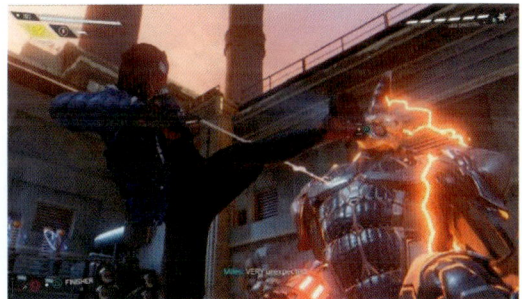

Forced into a one on one confrontation, Miles will now have a new trick up his sleeve - and it's the only way to take down this unstoppable force. Using R1+ Triangle, you can unleash a Venom Punch that will stun and briefly disable your opponents while doing massive damage. You can put this to great use by wailing on the boss for a combo hit while he can't fight back.

Your Venom Punch is tied to a new meter that builds as you attack and dodge - but against Rhino, you're better off building the meter using the latter. Most times your basic attacks will be useless and he'll instantly counter with a much harder hit, so stick to focusing on his swings and dodge out of the way - as it will not only raise the Venom Meter, but build your combo meter with successful dodges, allowing you to perform some instant takedowns as well.

Keep dancing around before unleashing a few Venom Punches, and Rhino will move things to a building interior.

Here, he'll start using charge attacks - but by dodging behind him, you can get on his back and steer him into a wall to briefly stun him. Try aiming for any electrical boxes, as they'll render him vulnerable to another beatdown without you having to worry about him swinging back.

Keep at it as you dodge his stomps, leaps, and swings until your meter is charged, and keep up the Venom Punches until he goes down, concluding the mission - and starting Miles Morales adventure.

Mission 2: Parting Gift

Location: Central Park

Rewards: 1,000 XP

Meet Ganke in Central Park

From your starting location in Harlem, swing south down into Central Park, and make your way towards a lone amphitheater in the park. Once you meet your pal Ganke, Miles will unlock a new spider suit - the Great Responsibility Suit.

Much like the previous Spider-Man game, Miles will be able to unlock a variety of suits over the course of his campaign. Some - like this suit - are unlocked by progressing the story, while others must be crafted from Activity and Tech Tokens, and you'll learn where to find those soon enough.

Certain suits also unlock special mods that you can equip to bolster your abilities, either as a suit mod or visor mode, but like certain suits - some of these must be crafted as well.

Once the suit's operating system boots up, Pete will promise an additional present at another location, finishing this mission and beginning the next one.

Mission 3: New Thwip

Location: Harlem

Rewards: 3,500 XP

Check Out Pete's Surprise

Following the signal sent out, swing your way up from Central Park to the northwest side of Harlem to find a small rooftop with a large spider symbol on top. Once there, look for a computer in the corner to access the program Pete has set up.

This will be your primer into the various holographic challenges that Peter has set up around New York for you to try out. Completing these in the categories of combat, stealth, and traversal will earn you Activity Tokens depending on your abilities.

As Peter runs you through the tutorial, you'll be able to try out some of Miles' more varied moves - like aerial combat. Sending enemies into the air is a huge advantage in combat, as it leaves your target vulnerable to more hits, and other melee opponents will be unable to reach you. Start off with an uppercut by holding down attack, then continue the assault while the hologram opponent is stunned. Remember that enemies with melee weapons will block

your most basic attacks unless you can launch them first.

Next up - employ a swing kick against the next hologram by holding down attack while you're already in mid-air. Use it on the next three enemies to send them flying and then finishing them off. After that, use your webs to disarm the next gun-toting opponent and keep them away from firearms. Then, use your webbing to slam down opponents in the air after knocking them up, and defeat the next group.

Holographic Peter will surprise you with an ambush, prompting you to use a Venom Punch Slam to clear the area - using up your Venom Meter in the process. Like the regular Venom Punch, it's a good way to give yourself some breathing room. You'll be tasked with defeating a few more holograph opponents with all kinds of weapons, so use what you've learned to disarm with your webs and then knock them into the air to isolate and finish them off.

Defeat the Thieves and Holograms

Just as the program is about to conclude, the program will start to malfunction - and to make matters worse, several thieves will appear with weapons to plunder Peter's computer tech. As they prepare to open fire, holograms will start to appear and also engage you, making the whole encounter pretty hectic.

Treat it like an expansion of the challenge simulation - dodge the gunfire, disarm them with web shots, and spin the weapons and other debris around to smash into thieves and holograms alike. You can also use some scaffolding against the far corner to bring down on a few heads as more enemies join the fray.

Remember to keep up on your dodging, as it builds your Venom Meter to unleash more big blows to clear a path and give yourself room to plan your next moves. Remember that with a few web shots you can get an opponent webbed up, and then perform a swing kick to launch them into a wall and stick them permanently.

Repair the Training Simulator

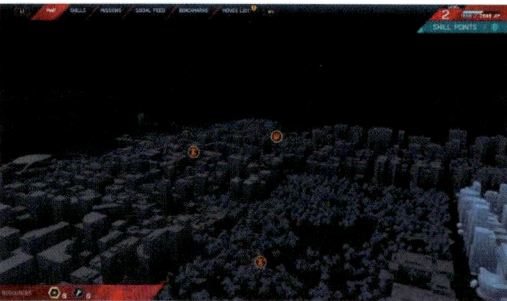

Once all holograms and thieves are taken care of, return to the computer in the corner to fix things up, and unlock challenges all across New York. As mentioned before, completing these challenges will earn your tokens to help build your suits, mods, and gadgets. Two such mods will be unlocked for your suit and visor, but you'll need a bunch of Activity Tokens to build them. Completing each of the training programs will also unlock exclusive skills that

shouldn't be missed.

With the mission complete, you can even engage in the real combat training at this location - challenging you to try and hit a record number of assailants with thrown items, and will unlock a longer spin move if you complete it. Go for the record using the Spin Cycle move you gain from the challenge, and you should earn enough tokens to build your first suit mod.

Mission 4: We're Here For You

Location: Harlem

Rewards: 3,500 XP

Investigate the Roxxon Plaza

From the challenge area you just completed, head east across Harlem towards the edge where the new Roxxon Plaza has been built, complete with the giant ominous orb in the middle of the plaza.

After getting the spiel from Simon Krieger, Miles will investigate a nearby broken window, and once inside, check out the computer at the far end of the room, only to be attacked by the unknown intruder.

Defeat the Intruders

These new enemies you'll face come armed with some seriously wild purple-tinted tech that allows them to form giant gauntlets and firearms alike. Just like armed opponents, the gauntlets will block direct attacks - but they'll also be immune to launching, at least from head-on attacks. Instead, use your Venom Punch to break their gauntlets to knock them down to size, and set about webbing up or disarming the ranged attackers to even the playing field. If you're lacking sufficient Venom Power, you can always dodge under them to attack from behind, or build up your meter by dodging and fighting others.

As more opponents appear on the roofs above, they may also toss down grenades. Luckily, like most everything else, you can quickly grab onto them and launch them right back at your attackers to deal some massive damage to a group at once. Note that their crazy tech can repair itself, so even disarming their shooters won't last forever.

Keep moving along rooftops as more appear until some nearby windows are broken, revealing more attackers inside one of the buildings. They'll try and hold you off as they access some files, but you priority is taking down every last one of them. Watch in particular for the enemies with the gauntlets as they can employ some ground pounding shockwave attacks you'll need to avoid, and stun them with thrown objects until you can break through their defenses or use a special takedown on them.

Continue beating them up as you move up the floors to higher levels, and watch for more incoming grenades and gunfire - and remember you can use a lot of objects in these rooms to throw back and smash your attackers with.

Investigate the Office

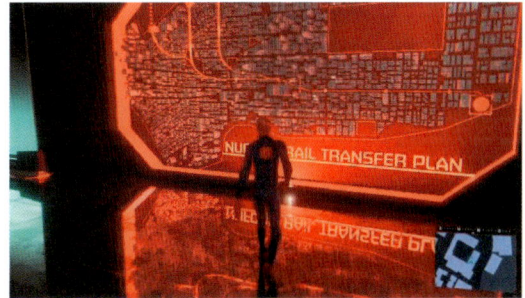

Once you've dealt with everyone here, look into the last office room where you faced the intruders to find a big red wall with the words Nuform Rail Transfer Plan, and investigate to find out what these mystery attackers were so keen on finding out about Roxxon. Wen Roxxon shows up to lock down the plaza, your task will be complete.

Mision 5: La Nochebuena

Location: Harlem

Rewards: 3,500 XP

Return Home and Head to the Kitchen

Head back to Miles' apartment - the one next to the large mural of Spider-Man you saw at the start of the game, and enter through the roof where your backpack full of clothes is waiting.

Once inside, you can inspect Miles' room to

find a few interesting items, like a tableside photo, ticket for a play, a very old TV, some of Miles costume design ideas, and more.

At the kitchen, Miles' mom will ask him to help out around the place and get everything ready for dinner. Start by turning on the Christmas tree near the table, and then check out the record player near the living room sofa. With no records to play, head down the hall to find some in Miles' mom's room. You can also check out your looks in the bathroom mirror, or check in on your pal Ganke in your room. While in mom's room, you can look out for a stack of newspapers, as well as a peculiar case file Miles' dad had worked on.

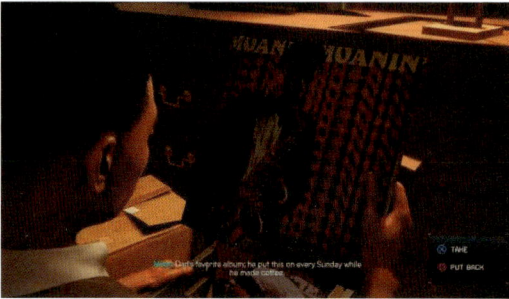

Select one of the vinyls to bring back to the record player, answer the door to reveal the surprise guest, and dinner can finally get started - until the power goes out.

Get the Power Back On

First things first, check out the circuit breaker at the end of the hall, but you'll have no luck. Head to your room and out onto the fire escape, where Miles will do a bit of investigating to find the transformer. He may not have his web shooters on, but he can still stick to walls just fine.

Move up towards the roof, but turn left at the end - since people are up there. Turn the corner on the building and move along until you need to dip down past your apartment windows to get around a billboard. Once past your family, go back up towards the top and keep moving left to find a generator you can interact with to restore power with your Venom Punch.

Head back along to your apartment's windows, and Ganke will run interference while you sneak back in. Now you can enjoy the rest of the Christmas Eve Dinner as the mission concludes.

Mission 6: Harlem Trains Out of Service

Location: Harlem

Rewards: 3,500 XP

Head to the Subway Stop

From your apartment, head east towards the Roxxon Plaza to find one of the Harlem train stops, and meet up with the operator who has a problem. You'll be told that a sensor relay over at Grand Central Station has gone offline, and someone may be interfering with it.

Travel south along the rail line all the way down to the other side of a very large building in Midtown to find the relay on a low roof over Grand Central - one of them is currently hooked up to a suspicious wire.

Use your spidey senses by pressing R3 to highlight the cable's path down onto a lower roof, around a corner into a gated area, and inside a small room with a locked double door. Tear it down to find a member of the Underground working on a computer, and quickly zip over to him and put him out of commission.

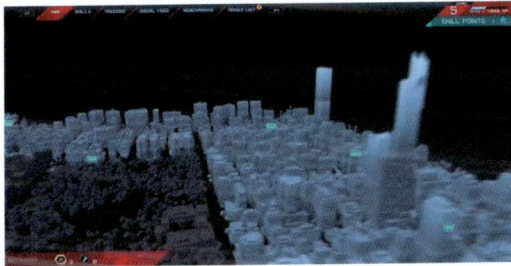

Inspect the computer to disable the jamming device, and Miles will also find a crate full of Underground tech, giving you a Tech Token - which you can find more of all over New York. Using Tech Tokens along with Activity Tokens will let you unlock new suits, mods, and gadgets- like Holo Drone fighters to mess with your opponents.

Defeat the Underground Thugs

As you move to leave the room, you'll be ambushed by a host of Underground goons, including those with the heavy gauntlets and rifles. Try out those new Holo Drones by selecting them on your gadget list using R1, and use them to run interference while you disarm the rifle users, and toss any grenades right back at them.

Search the Rail Yard

After taking out the enemy group, you'll get word that more activity has been reported at a rail yard over in Hell's Kitchen to the west. Make your way over there, but be sure to check out any nearby Underground Caches along the way to score some more tech tokens. There's one in an alley below the large Ellie Jude Hotel sign under some scaffolding you can tear down to get into.

As you arrive, you'll find even more Underground loitering around, which is your chance to add a little stealth to your moves. When highlighting an enemy in these conditions, you'll see an indicator for whether another enemy will notice if you try for a silent takedown. When multiple people are about, look for objects to thwip some webbing at to attract attention, and then web up the remaining thug while the others are distracted. You can also perform a zip takedown using triangle on the second guy, but remember these are much louder and should be used sparingly.

Once on top of the train, be sure to take a careful look around and mark all available targets by holding down L2. Cross reference the targets with your minimap to make sure everyone is accounted for - like the guy on the balcony by the building, and the lone person working on the generator near where you took out the first target.

A good general rule of thumb is to take out isolated targets first - starting with higher ground targets like the one on the balcony. After he's out of the picture, grab the one working on the generator around the corner, and then wait for the two under the balcony to separate.

Next, work on isolating the small groups by the trains. Even if you haven't been detected, there's a good chance that they'll become suspicious when people fail to check in, but this may work to your favor as they split up to investigate.

You should also note the crane in the far corner you can yank to pull down debris on two thugs below, taking them out instantly and without exposing yourself. There's also a larger garbage dumpster on wheels you can drag out to ram into a few of them.

Get the Trains Back in Service

With the thugs taken care of, zip back up to the balcony and enter the door to find the train controls have been sabotaged. Miles will need to take matters into his own hands, using webs to get the job done.

Start by zipping over to the post near the turntable the first train is on, and press L1+R1 on one of the corners to spin it around. Do this until the train is facing the rail access tunnel, and then zip down in front of it to pull the train directly into the tunnel, clearing space on the turntable.

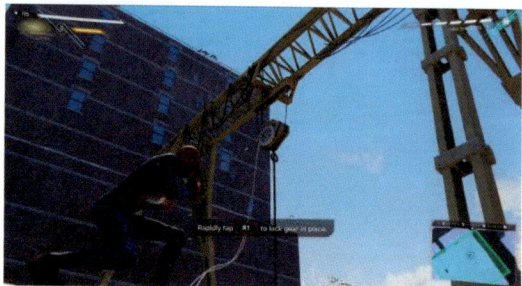

Next, look at the far end past the turntable for a train that's high in the air, and zip up to it to find a gear you can pull on to set the train down - but it won't last forever. Get things to stay in place by quickly gumming up the gear with a few web shots after pulling it down, and leave it where it is.

Finally, head back near the turntable and spin it so that it's facing the only train that's perpendicular to the other trains, and pull this train onto the turntable, and spin it once more so the three trains are now back to back.

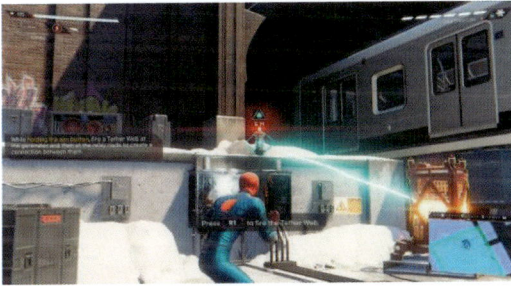

To power the whole rail line up, look at the busted generator one of the thugs was sabotaging near the rail line, and then turn your attention to the nearby red generator. Power it up with your Venom Punch, and then zoom in on the powered generator to fire a tethered web from the generator to the red light above the electrical line.

Return to the East Harlem Station

With the rail line active and your job done, soar above the buildings back up from Midtown to Harlem to meet back with Aaron at the Harlem Line. Be sure to keep an eye out for any more Underground Cache locations on the way back - there are some on abandoned rooftops and at the entrance to the old Fisk Tower.

As you get near the station, you'll get word that the Underground isn't too happy with how you handled things, and are setting bombs around the station. They'll be in a protracted battle against the police under the raised rail line when you get there, with a bomb located by a fence nearby.

You'll have around a minute before the first bomb detonates, so try to clear the area first, and use Holo Drones to run interference and then yank the bomb into the air when nobody is trying to hit you. Rapidly tap on your web shooter to web it up as it explodes, and then get ready to find the next bomb.

Head up onto the raised tracks themselves to find the next bomb, along with a couple of more thugs. Try using swing kicks and your Venom Punch to clear the raised area, and knock them off to give yourself a clear shot at grabbing the bomb and disposing of it.

Finally, head back under to find two more bombs and even more thugs. The ones with the gauntlets can make getting an uninterrupted shot of the bombs hard, so utilize Venom Punches and special takedowns to get them out of the way early, and web up any others that stand in your way while you disable the last bombs. After that, clean up anyone still standing to complete the mission.

Finishing this Friendly Neighborhood Spider-Man App will reward you with a bunch of Activity Tokens, so make use of them to craft yourself some new suits or mods! You'll have some time until the next main mission, so you can also participate in more activities and a new side quest in Harlem until then. There's also crime in progress you can stop - like in the first game, completing extra side objectives will gain you more activity tokens.

Mission 7: Reconnecting

Location: Upper West Side

Rewards: 1,500 XP

Meet with Phin

This mission is pretty much just a cutscene, so make your way over to the Upper West Side from Harlem, and be sure to take on any activities or stop crime on your way over, earning more Activity Tokens, and plundering Underground Caches for Tech Tokens.

Once you reach the building Phin wants to meet at, you'll find it near the waterfront behind a large Ellie James Hotel sign on a lower section of the roof where you can discreetly enter a door and change.

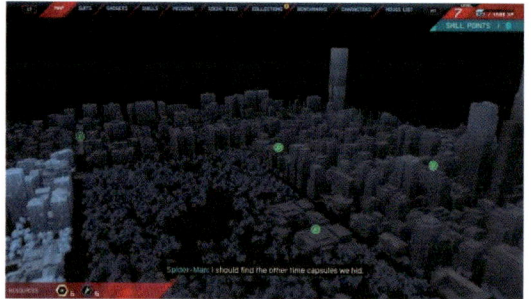

After the cutscene concludes, you'll be alerted to Time Capsules located all over New York. Like the backpack collectibles in the first Spider-Man game, you'll be able to hunt down these items to earn some extra Activity Tokens. For now, the mission will conclude as you head back home for the day - activating fast travel locations, including one that goes right to your house.

Mission 8: Time to Rally

Location: Harlem

Rewards: 4,000 XP

Reach the Rally

As you and Ganke leave the apartment, take in the sights of the street fair as you make your way down the long street towards the site of Miles' mom's rally stand. There's a couple of street vendors and an artist you can talk to along the way.

Be sure to use your spidey senses by pressing R3 to highlight things you can interact or talk to. You can even catch your Uncle hanging about near the site of the rally and talk to him.

After the speech concludes, it'll be time to get to work as Spider-Man, so get ready!

Defeat the Underground

You'll have to engage a group of thugs that include a gauntlet user and some ranged support, so dodge the initial attacks and use nearby debris to fling into their face as you charge up a Venom Punch to disable the melee attacker.

More attackers will appear on the nearby construction yard's low rooftops, and it's best to quickly zip to the ledges and dive into your attackers. If you've picked up skills like Venom Jump and Web Yank, you can try launching multiple opponents into the air, knock them away, and yank them back to deal a bunch of damage.

Keep your eyes up for incoming fire from the different rooftops, and do your best to disarm and neutralize them by grabbing weapons and hurling back grenades.

Head to the Explosion and Stop the Underground

Once you clear out the enemies at the rally, an explosion will alert you to the Underground's real plans on the nearby bridge. Swing over as fast as you can to intercept the attackers on the western bridge.

After an explosive cutscene, the bridge will be in bad shape, but it wont stop a horde of Underground enemies from converging on you. Hopefully you've leveled up to the point where you have to uses of the Venom Bar now, as it will come in handy for clearing crowds. Use the Slam or Jump if you get surrounded, and the punch to break down those pesky gauntlets.

More Underground will show up on top of cars, so be ready to evade gunfire and toss car doors at their faces, or fling grenades back at them.

Save the Civilians

After defeating enough of the Underground, part of the bridge will start collapsing, and you'll need to help those still trapped on the bridge before it's too late.

As soon as you regain control of Miles, zip to the ledge on the bridge where a group of people are, and use L1+R1 on the water tanker truck to douse the flames blocking their escape. As you jump away, you can spot a bus nearby teetering on the edge. Zip down in front of it and aim at the front wheels to launch a volley of webbing to keep it from tipping over, then web the front by pressing triangle. When it starts to fall, mash square and press triangle once more to save the last passenger.

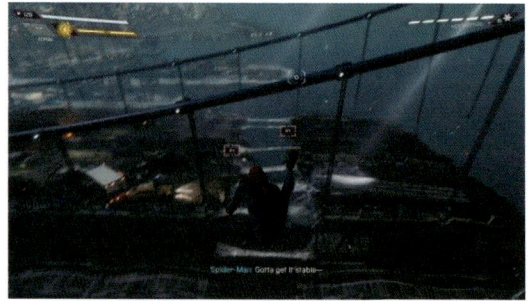

As you launch back upwards another section of the bridge will break, trapping more people between a gap. Jump up and rapidly hit R1 to web it up, then zip over to the opposite side of the bridge from the survivors. Look for a nearby truck bed to yank across and create a platform for the people to run across, and mash square to keep it in place.

After reducing the last person, Roxxon will show up, and Miles will be forced to beat a hasty retreat with some newfound powers, concluding the mission.

After things settle down, you'll find you now have the ability to camouflage both in and out of combat by pressing up on the D-Pad. This lets you move unseen to strike without warning, though there is a lengthy cooldown once you reappear before you can use it again. Keep it in mind for future encounters!

Mission 9 : Someone Left the Lights On

Location: Greenwich

Rewards: 4,500 XP

Find a Way Inside the Shop

Make your way down Manhattan to the southwest side where Greenwich is, and look for a small store behind a blue market with the sign Mason's Repair. You'll need to find a way in the boarded up place, and a nearby roof tower window seems the best option.

Inside, you can take your time to explore the abandoned shop and check out some of the forgotten items, like some guitars, a framed dollar, and a backpack. In the back of the shop, you'll find a table of interesting clues you can zoom in and examine, like a fake ID card, the Nuform Development Team list.

On a nearby kitchen table, you find some

medicine - but the real secret is behind a small brick wall glowing with purple, so use your Venom Smash to investigate.

Inside the secret room, you can check out some of the workbenches to find some Underground gear, and then finally look on the nearby computer for more clues.

Defeat the Underground

Trouble will show up, as it usually does, but this time you'll be able to start employing limited camouflage to get away from danger. Press up on the D-Pad and zip to a vantage point first, then wait for a sniper to take the high ground overlooking the alley, and zip up behind him to take him out.

If you get spotted again, you can always camouflage and hide until they stop becoming aware of your presence - otherwise, get behind the other two snipers and go into camo mode to take them out from behind.

More snipers will appear on the hardware store roof as you fight the remaining thugs - which may be a good time to stealth again as you zip up to their level. Either wait for them to relax or use your invisibility to get the first strike and shut them down if possible. Camouflage drains quickly when attacking, but at a much slower rate if you stay relatively still and hide behind enemies.

Once the group is defeated, return to the computer to get the location of the phone that was lost, and you'll have the destination of your next mission set.

Mission 10: Corporate Espionage

Location: Chinatown

Rewards: 4,500 XP

Infiltrate the Lab

Swing on down to Chinatown to find one of the Roxxon labs - you can't miss the black and red design of the building. There's only one entrance, and it's shielded, so you'll need to get rid of the nearby guards.

There are three outside, including one with a powerful melee weapon, so sneak attack him and then disable his friends quickly. In order

to lower the vent shields, use R3 to find the connecting power supply and rip open the case, then overload it by holding L1 and tapping square to absorb its energy.

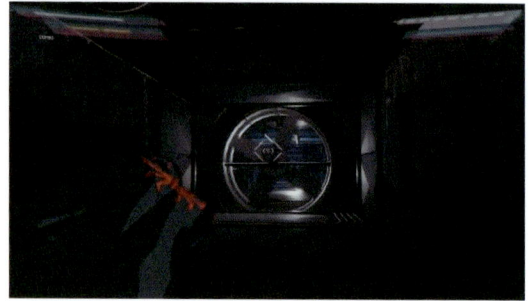

As you crawl inside, you'll be met with some obstacles in the form of spinning fans. Aim your web shooter and gum up the fans to slip through, and crawl down to a lower level. When you reach an intersection with three spinning fans, take the left path, as the others will lead you in a circle.

You'll drop out into a flooded room full of pipes, so hop across the water to a crack in the wall on the other side to squeeze through, then descend down the long drop to the level below.

Almost instantly, the door behind you will begin to open, so trigger your camouflage to avoid the patrol of Roxxon security as they move through the room. You actually don't have to engage them at all - just make sure they don't bump into you as you move into a corner of the room behind their path.

Find the Phone

Once they've left, enter the hall they came from to run into an unexpected ally. Once this new friend agrees to help you out, you'll

Once they've left, enter the hall they came from to run into an unexpected ally. Once this new friend agrees to help you out, you'll receive some Remote Mines. These items can be thrown to emit a burst of electricity to incapacitate a nearby target - but can also be thrown at electrical outlets to expand their reach to hit multiple targets, and can even be thrown on an enemy to shock them.

With your new gadget, slip through the nearby vent to a room full of Roxxon security, and look for a fuse box on the floor to toss your mine on, and detonate it to shock up to three enemies at once.

As their friends move to investigate, zip crash into the guard alone at the top of the stairs, then turn back to either silently (or loudly) take out the remaining guards. Once they're dealt with, look up to the right wall to find a vent above a door you can zip into.

After witnessing a short and interesting scene, crawl through the passage and up a slope into a larger room full of more security guards. You can kick things off by waiting for a guard to walk left to another at a control console, and toss a remote mine at the fuse box in front of them - catching a third guard not far away. This way, you can zip up to the

light fixtures over them and pick off the Roxxon guards who come to investigate their bodies one by one. After they've been taken care of, check out the terminal they were using to unlock the sites of several other Roxxon Labs you can take on later to earn Activity Tokens.

Zip through the open window in front of the terminal to find the large room with the fan where the phone has been lost. There are several snipers here posted along the catwalks, so start at the top and wait for the guards that patrol between them to leave the snipers exposed to getting webbed up silently. There's two snipers and two patrollers on the top level - it's a good idea to take time to mark up all your targets to track them as they move around the fan, and snatch the snipers first when the others are out of sight.

Moving down to the next level, there's 5 more guards here, but thankfully no snipers. Look for the guards that patrol along the outer ring and leave themselves isolated from their friends to pick them off first, then circle around back to the inner circle where the others who don't move around are - and distract any who are grouped up to divide and conquer them carefully. Even if there are no electrical fuse boxes here, you can still toss a mine onto an enemy's back and disable them from a distance - which can prove to be highly useful if you hit another enemy at the same time.

In order to stop the fan long enough for you to get to the phone, you'll need to drop down to a catwalk just above the fan blades and look for a large gear you can yank to reveal a bunch of wiring. Web up the gears after pulling, then yank on the wires to turn the fan off - and hop down to grab the phone.

Disable the Nuform Reactor

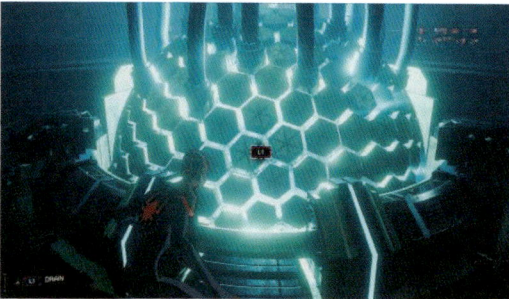

After learning the horrible truth about Roxxon's secrets, Miles will have a change of plans. After your ally reluctantly agrees to help, swing back up to the platforms above as the shields around the reactor are raised. Just like the generator outside, grab on with L1 and mash square to try and absorb all of its energy.

Your health and venom meter will start fluctuating, so you'd better get moving and head down the hall. Thankfully, by the time you reach a wall to climb up, your health will start stabilizing, and you can swing up to the room above.

Escape the Lab

A Roxxon Shield Guard will appear to attack you. Pay attention when these guys enter a room - as trying to use a Venom Punch or similar venom-infused direct attack will be absorbed by their shields, and promptly redirected at you. In order to render them vulnerable, you'll need to grab onto their shield with your webs, or get in close and perform a Venom Jump to get them into the air where they can't defend themselves.

They'll also use powerful slamming attacks with their shields, and can send bursts of energy your way or charge at you extremely fast, so be ready to take them out as soon as you see them in a fight. If they toss grenades your way, throw them back to stun them, or build up your combo meter on the other guards so you can take them out with a special takedown. If they manage to hit you with their grenades or shockwave attacks, you'll be unable to use any venom-based powers for a short while, so avoid the waves from their shockwaves whenever possible.

After taking them out, you'll meet up with your ally, only to get ambushed in a room full of various Roxxon guards. You'll have help now, but you shouldn't take this fight lightly, as you'll be surrounded on all sides. Including the Shield Guards, you'll also have to contend with rocket launchers, and close quarters fighters.

In particular, the Roxxon guards in green and red can be tricky, as they can disengage from combat when you're trying to perform a combo attack by rolling away and pulling out a pistol for a quick shot. As long as you're ready for this counter, you can drive them back and be ready to perform a perfect dodge to keep them stunned.

Since your ally will usually be concerned with taking out the foes on the ground level, it'll be worth your while to zip up to the armed guards on the upper levels, as well as those with the rocket launchers. You can also utilize your camo to give yourself a brief respite as they focus attention on your partner and let you sneak up on your targets.

As more and more waves of enemies appear, you'll be alerted to beat a hasty retreat - once your camera shifts to an explosion in the wall, quickly zip through before you're overwhelmed. With the mission concluded, you'll have a bit of time before the next one appears, so feel free to investigate those other Roxxon Labs - which function much like the gang hideouts in the other Spider-Man game.

Mission 11: Underground Undercover

Location: Hell's Kitchen

Rewards: 4,500 XP

Meet Phin in Hell's Kitchen

Once Miles works up the nerve to call up his friend, you'll need to meet up a bit south of Fisk Tower at the top corner of Hell's Kitchen that borders Central Park. Look for a door on a nearby roof to go in so you can change and meet up.

When she takes you to another high rise building, follow her up the side of the building and up a series of ledges until you come to a large crane leading to Fisk Tower. You'll have to play the part of meek little Miles Morales - but don't worry about falling or missing the jump.

Gather Clues About the Nuform

Once you get across, you'll be deep in Underground territory. Follow your friend in and inspect a sword on a nearby table (expect to see this weapon again in the future). Once you're relatively alone, it's time to start searching around for clues.

Move past the crowd into the larger room with the large graffiti screen of Fisk, and be sure to inspect the screen as well as the various tables of weapons and armor the Underground has gained in the last few months. Over on the other side some Underground are watching news reports of their exploits you can tune into, as well as plenty of cash - and a clue to where more treasures may be stored.

Finally, head out onto the balcony at the far end to progress things along. After the leader dives down to the lobby below, you'll need to follow - but in another change of clothes.

Locate the Nuform

Enter the vents once you've got your suit on to end up in a training yard where Fisk Tower's lobby used to be. There's enemies everywhere - including plenty of snipers patrolling around the upper ledges. Grab up the sniper below you, and then take the time to scan the room and mark targets - including the people fighting the training dummies below you, the firing range on the far side, and the different snipers at various levels all around the room.

Take the high ground first to get around the side behind the top snipers and slowly work your way down. Make sure to keep track of where snipers move from side to side so you don't get spotted (or camo first before getting close).

When you get to the last group overlooking the training dummies, you'll need to distract the pair to separate them first (unless you have the skill upgrade to take out multiple enemies with one zip takedown). As you survey the ground floor, note the different things you can use - like scaffolds to pull down or electrical fuse boxes to rig with remote bombs. If you get spotted, you may want to consider camouflaging and ducking around a corner until they lose your position.

Expect more reinforcements to appear even if you aren't actually spotted - once someone notices a remote bomb trigger or some webbing, other may appear from some of the balconies or dropping in from above, so always be aware of your surroundings so you don't get hit from behind when you least expect it.

When all the Underground forces and reinforcements are dealt with, you'll need to find the entrance to a secret chamber. After getting a clue from Ganke, head along the lobby to the boarded up front entrance to find a giant samurai statue holding a sword. Yank the sword with your webs and you'll uncover a secret staircase going below.

Once you take the elevator down to the vaults, zip up into a grate and follow a group of Underground down a hall, and into the main vault. You'll learn about even more Underground hideouts, and a clue to the whereabouts of the Nuform itself. Before you can escape with your intel, you'll be attacked by more Underground - including a sword wielder.

Leave Fisk Tower

Sword wielders can be a pain to deal with. They'll use the extending blade to keep from being juggled in the air, and will dodge many of your attacks, including swing kicks and most Venom moves like Punches and Jumps. Even worse, these enemies can transform their weapons into whips to grab you right out of the air, and can attack from a much larger distance than you may think - dealing a ton of damage if they catch you unaware.

Instead, you'll unlock the Venom Dash to match their speed and slam into them, throwing them hard after an attack. This can be used to great effect to mow down groups of opponents in a line, and you'll need it to defeat these sword-wielders. Still, you can also use certain gadgets to slow them down like webbing and gravity wells.

Press the attack on the first sword wielder, but be ready for two more to appear from the vaults. They have pretty serious sword swing combos you need to dodge individually, but can also try and throw their sword whips at range if you aren't paying attention. Remember that holo drones can also distract their attention to give you time to set up a Venom Dash into them.

When all of the enemies are dealt with down in the vault, you can spy into the different chambers to see what Fisk - and now the Underground - have been hoarding, and then escape through a rear entrance by using the panel nearby, sending you out through a secret exit and completing the mission.

Mission 12: Curtain Call

Location: Upper East Side

Rewards: 5,000 XP

Disable the Generators

Swinging up into the Upper East Side to find the Gem Theater, you'll find the place locked up with an electrified roof access, and plenty of Underground swarming around the nearby buildings. Since the power to the door is supplied by nearby generators, you'll need to take out the Underground guarding the nearby spots.

Starting with the first generator to the north, swing up behind the sniper on the taller left roof and quietly take them out, then survey the rest below. There's six patrolling near the generator, with another sniper on the far side you should eliminate next.

Most of the other thugs here are in groups of two, but some will patrol away from their partners, and the others can be lured away with a web shot behind the large vertical platforms. Pick them off or just crash into the remaining few, and then grab onto the generator to drain its power.

Head to the center to the large recessed area below the theater next, where more snipers are covering the low area where another generator is being guarded. Take out the two snipers on either side of the ledges by zipping to the lamp posts above them.

Then, you can either try to lure some of the Underground to the scaffolding and pull it down on them, or just toss a remote mine at one of them to shock a few, and slam into the rest.

Some of the thugs are on slightly lower levels, and you can crawl along the walls under them and web them up from below when they peer over the ledges.

Next up is the south side on a higher rooftop opposite the north area, where plenty more Underground are patrolling the long roof where the generator stands. There's around nine to contend with, but thankfully no snipers, which means you can go in swinging if you prefer. Just be on the lookout for sword-wielders, as they are best taken out first while you're still undetected. However you engage them, make use of the plentiful debris, and lure some near scaffolding to topple it over their heads.

Disable the final generator, and back to the gate to use a Venom Smash to get inside.

As you crash land inside, you'll need to find a new way to get to the main hall. Look to the right to spy an elevator you can lift by yanking on a gear, then webbing it up to keep it in place. Once you drop into the main theater hall, you'll find the Nuform protected by a giant armored container.

Charge the Generators to Access the Nuform

Finally, head east to the highest rooftops over the theater to find the last generator. Go to the higher of the two buildings to find a sniper guarded by a sword-wielder, and take them out quietly, then head down to where the generator is.

In order to power up the container and open it up, you'll need to charge up several generators connected to the center, and it will require a bit of exploring.

25

From the terminal, look left to see a cable that has a small gap before crossing to the back of the theater and into a side room. Enter the room, and check out the box full of weapons and armor, and then charge up the nearby generator with a Venom Punch. It doesn't have any cables attached, so instead shot a tethered web from the generator to the isolated cable, and again towards the cable attached to the container to power this portion up.

From the generator you powered up, head up the small slope to another generator by a desk full of notes about Rick's invention, and power this one up too. It won't need any connecting, so you'll be good to go here.

Head to main stage of the theater to find a large backdrop blocking a generator against the back wall up some stairs, below a desk full of bad intel the Underground has been giving Roxxon. Look around using R3 to find a pulley

you can yank and web up to raise the backdrop, giving you a clear connecting line to shoot webbing from the generator.

Before moving on, check the far corner for more intel on a workbench desk, and then look behind you for a weak wall that's hiding an Underground Cache you can plunder.

Finally, head up to the balcony and follow a cable to a weak wall with the Underground logo, and break it apart to find the last generator next to a table with some pictures of yourself. The generator is embedded in the floor, so use a Venom Smash to hit the area below you and charge the last generator.

Defeat the Underground

Before you can pull off the heist, Underground thugs will convene into the theater and start patrolling the large area. You'll need to take them out - and there are plenty of ways to do so stealthily.

There's lots of light fixtures that can be found all over the theater to give you vantage points - use them to get behind lone patrolling guards and web them up without anyone noticing, starting at the back of the room and working your way forward.

When you encounter the larger groups, you can still keep things quiet but let them know you're around by leaving webs (or they'll start to notice missing people) and will start spreading out to search. That's your cue to keep tabs on the group by marking them, and follow those that isolate themselves away from the others. When they move to higher levels with no vantage spots, camo behind them to take them out quietly. You can also scope out fuse boxes to lure enemies into and shock larger groups.

If it gets to the point where you may get spotted, try eliminating the sword wielders first, as they'll be the biggest pain to deal with when the fighting breaks out. Know that regardless of your methods, the reinforcements will burst through after the initial group is gone and engage you directly.

A new fighter will appear among them, the Underground version of a Brute that wields a massive shield and hammer. The shield will allow them to do fast ramming charge attacks, as well as sweeping hits ending in a large area of effect slam.

Thankfully unlike the Roxxon shield users, they can't absorb a Venom Punch, and it will cause their shield to break. Unfortunately, doing this will get them pretty mad, and go all in on offense with their giant weapon. This can come in the form of massive ranged attacks, and sweeping combo swings that make them dangerous to be around.

You'll need to be equally as aggressive in breaking down their shield and then pressing the attack to keep them stunned and off-balance before they can start swinging. If you let them run around for too long, they'll eventually revert back to using a shield which you'll need to break again.

Stop the Tinkerer

After defeating the Brute and their companions, return to the Nuform - only to have the Tinkerer take it first and flee.

You'll need to give chase along the streets of Manhattan, similar to how you had to track down Rhino earlier on. She'll cause explosions to rain down everywhere. You don't have to worry about most of these, but if you see energy forming around the Tinkerer herself, that means she's about to launch a rocket at you - so be ready for the targeting indicator to appear and dodge while keeping up your momentum.

Follow her along to the edge of Central Park until you can tackle her, but she'll take off running again along the streets, sending cars flying as he goes. Continue to keep pace low to the ground using short swings and zips as she heads out to the docks, and be ready on those dodges when you start having less things to swing from getting close to the ships.

Once you start wall running on one of the ships, keep moving forward until you near a crane to jump off and swing back to land, and follow her to a building and run straight up.

She'll start sending a variety of spinning blades down your way - be ready to jump over the entire rows of blades, and move left or right around the single blades until you reach the top.

Once the scene is over, the mission will conclude, and Miles will need to get some advice on what to do next. You'll have some time before the next mission, so feel free to complete a few side missions and activities until then.

Mission 13: Breaking Through the Noise

Location: Hell's Kitchen

Rewards: 5,000 XP, 5 Activity Tokens

Meet Uncle Aaron in Hell's Kitchen

After waiting awhile and taking on some side missions, Aaron will ask you to meet over by the docks in Hell's Kitchen, not far from where you had to race along boats chasing the Tinkerer. After a lengthy cutscene, Aaron will suggest you take time to relax and sample the noises of the city to develop a beat.

Sample the Correct Noise

Once you interact with the hologram of the audio device, you'll be able to pull up an audio sample of something in the vicinity of your area. As you hold down L2, you'll hear directional audio of many things around you, and pressing triangle will let you listen to the beat of something specific nearby.

Your job is to find whatever source is matching that original sample, and record it. For this interaction, the beat takes the form of two distinct bell noises. From the hologram point, zip up to the poles above, then turn right to find a bright red buoy. Zip over to the storage containers overlooking the buoy, then hold L2 while looking at it. When prompted, record the new clean sample over the old one that matches to correctly identify the source.

At this point, a new collectible will become available around the city as you uncover more audio samples and earn more Activity Tokens. Otherwise, Miles will be ready to enact a plan and take off, and a new day will begin.

Note that when you wake up, Miles will have somehow made a lot of progress in decorating his room, and there's more to find and interact with in the apartment before you leave.

Mission 14: Tinker Tailor Soldier Spy

Location: Financial District

Rewards: 6,000 XP

Deciding to throw caution to the wind, Miles plans to meet with the Tinkerer face to face to try and avoid further needless confrontation, and find a mutual way to stop Roxxon without endangering lives. However, someone else knows about the meeting, which may throw everyone's plans into chaos.

Find a Way Out

After being attacked, use your newfound power to unleash a Mega Venom Blast by pressing L1, circle, and triangle. This ability

costs three full venom bars to perform, but it will send everything around you flying for days.

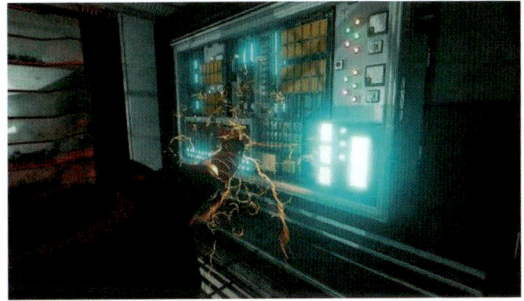

Once you've regained control, follow Phin into the next room and access a computer to find a way out through several offices and a control room. When the door leading out is locked, look up to slip through a vent and crawl to a small generator and Venom Punch it to power the door and open up a path forward.

Once you reach the main office room, you'll need to help Phin get across by playing things safe - or smashing everything in sight. Remember you can crawl along the ceiling and web up those under you if nobody else is watching. Yank up the Roxxon guard nearest Phin, then move towards the big monitors past his position to where two guards are talking, and a third patrols between them and more guards on the other side of the room.

You only need to take out the two guards by the monitor for Phin to do her thing, so you can wait until the patroller moves off and ping a nearby desk with some webbing so one investigates, grab his friend, and then the one who comes back from investigating.

After she hacks the first terminal, you'll need to access teh door, but more guards will appear nearby to station themselves around Phin. She needs to get all the way to the far corner, which means the rest of the guards likely need to disappear to make that happen.

You can still keep webbing up more of them on the ceiling by drawing them apart and pinging desks with webs. However, the last two guards stationed in the middle are under a lower ceiling, so to get them you may want to toss a mine at one of them, shock him, and zip to his companion before he can act.

Trigger the Override

As Phin works on the door, she'll ask you to help trigger the override in a terminal you can find in an adjacent room. The office area is actually full of several monitors you can interact with to get some audio logs from Simon Krieger, providing insight into his motives.

You can also find an Underground Cache to get a free Tech Part from (Phin will understandably be annoyed at this). After checking out all the terminals to get some clues, trigger the override with Phin and exit the room. You'll get a big revelation during the next cutscene, after which you'll need to continue your escape.

Access the Control Room

Head along the underground grate until you reach a dead end, and use your powers to disable a nearby generator keeping it shut.

In the next room, you'll need to find a way to bring the power back on and get inside the control room. While Phin gets to an access panel, take scope of the room to spy a nearby generator, an assembly line in the middle, a moveable crane arm on the far side, and below it - an engine.

Power up the generator with a Venom Punch, and the crane will move into the middle. Hop over to the far side next to the engine, and yank the crane over to hang above, while Phin grabs it. Yank it back to the middle, and she'll place the engine on the assembly line - but the laser power will short out.

In order to power the laser, you need to move some electricity from the generator to the red electrical rod near where the engine was first found - but its behind a panel. To circumvent this, attach a web line from the generator to the top of the crane. Yank the crane back to the far side once it is carrying a current, and then connect the line from the crane to the red note to power things up.

Finally, power up the engine now that it's been imbued by using a Venom Punch, then grab it with your webs and toss it at the blast shields to open a path to the control room.

Defeat the Enemies

While Phin tries to open up an escape route, it will be up to you to clear out the Roxxon guards in the next room. Note the guys with the blue visors - they'll see you even if you try and camouflage, so try to attack from vantage points using stealth for as long as you can. Even with their goggles, they hardly look up, so

focus on taking them out first while they remain unaware of your presence.

Start by moving above the central catwalk and taking out the goggles guard and his friends as they patrol in separate directions. From there, look to the back right of the room where a lone guard with the goggles is looking around, and pick him off while he's isolated (or bring down a fan on him).

As you head back across to the catwalk under where you entered, note that there are a few cranes holding objects you can trigger to fall on the heads of the guards below - use them to sow distraction as you pick off targets who are distracted by the commotion.

You can also make some of the lasers along the assembly line go haywire and attack nearby enemies. Don't worry - as long as they don't physically detect you, they won't sound an alarm. If they do, they'll call for several reinforcements - which can make things a lot harder if you're going for a straight-on fight.

If you play your cards right, Phin will gain access without Roxxon even noticing, and you can slip through a vent above the far window after cleaning up the rest. Otherwise you may have to battle it out for a bit first. When you're ready, head into the showroom floor and across into Krieger's Lab.

Defeat the Boss

As things get crazy, you'll go toe to toe with an old foe, who's found a way around your signature Venom strikes. As Phin handles the Roxxon guards, focus your attention on defeating the big guy.

In order to lower his defenses to your Venom, you'll need to tear off his new armor piece by piece, and that involves slamming him into things to stun him - namely, the large APC vehicles displayed around the showroom floor. Wait for him to charge at you, dodge behind him, and steer him right into one to stun him.

When he goes town, unleash a flurry of blows (but not Venom blows) to chip away at his armor. However, you can use Special Takedowns to do a bit of extra damage during these moments. Don't let up your assault and don't worry about anyone else during these sequences.

In between the periods when he's stunned, you'll need to carefully wait out his next charge attack. He may stomp around and swipe at you, or even toss rubble your way - and you may have to dodge incoming fire from Roxxon guards while you wait, but don't take your eyes off him. You can however use his unstoppable charge to mow down some unsuspecting guards - just make sure you hit an APC vehicle at the end so he gets stunned.

After you knock off a lot of his armor, he'll get really mad, and start hurling the APCs at you so you can't ram him into them. Using what you learned back at the assembly bay however, you can charge up the engines after he breaks them down to supercharge the engines - and toss one in his face. Just be wary of his increased stomp attacks, as they'll send three trails of shockwaves that can hurt and stop you from using your abilities.

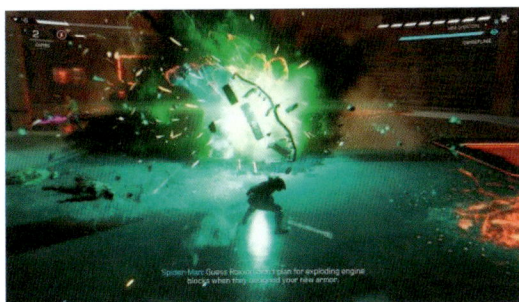

Keep up the dodging, and be sure to wait to toss the engine until after his stomp to get those shots in. Once another scene happens, his Roxxon upgrades will have broken off, and you'll be free to engage. Now would be a great time to utilize that Mega Venom Burst to stun both Rhino and any nearby Roxxon soldiers to boot, giving you plenty of room to smack him around all over the place.

You can even continue to dodge over his charge, ride him into an APC to stun him, beat him down, and follow up with a quick Venom Punch to keep him stunned and prevent him from getting back on his feet.

As long as you keep that pressure up, the boss will fall before you in no time. However, not everything goes as planned, and while the mission will be complete, the fight will not be over.

Like the last mission, you'll be able to relax in Miles' apartment and check out the new items before heading out once more, and take out some more crime until the next mission becomes available.

Mission 15: Thicker Than Blood

Location: Upper West Side

Rewards: 5,000 XP

Defeat the Boss

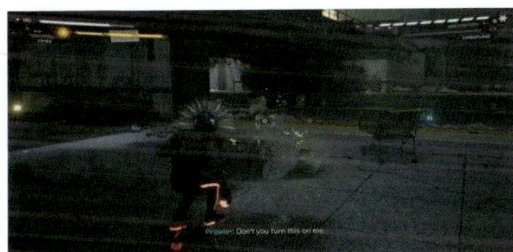

This enemy is unlike any you've fought before. What will start as a simple beatdown will get confusing as your target vanishes after getting hit a few times. Instead, you'll need to be safe, and patient. Listen with your spidey sense, and look for an incoming attack to dodge and counter. As you continue to do this, you'll even be able to get in a few venom attacks or special takedowns if you're careful to deal even more damage.

Certain times however, he may appear at a distance and form a giant green shield to dash at you with, which can be dodged and give you a brief moment to zip after him to follow up.

Speaking of which, having the mods to increase your perfect dodge window and deal more damage afterwards can really help web his face if you react to his incoming attacks and give you more time to fight back each time.

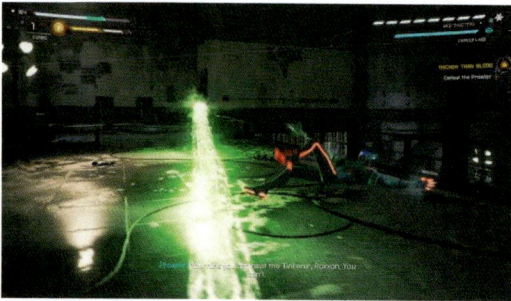

Once he gets hit back a few times, he'll take his claws out and upgrade his fighting style. At this point you need to be ready, as he'll appear with less warning to unleash giant beams of energy that can come with little warning.

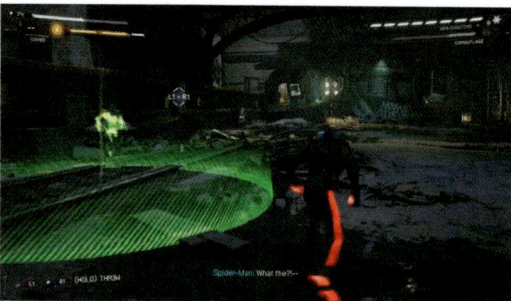

He may also toss out multiple grenades that can suppress your Venom powers. Speaking of which, all Venom strikes can help stun him if you catch him unaware (though he'll quickly get out of a Venom Jump)

If you find yourself in need of a boost, you can try camouflaging to give him the slip and look for generators along the lower walls you can absorb energy from.

Counter his moves enough times, and he'll change up his tactics yet again - employing holographic clones to confuse you. They can't disappear like he can, but they use a lot of his moves at a slower pace that can still make it hard to single him out.

A good strategy here is to keep dodging the attacks supplied by him and his clones to build your venom meter, then attack back with a Venom Slam or even a Mega Venom Burst to catch everyone at once and deal massive damage, eliminating all the clones in one hit. Just keep your eye out for those quick acting grenades, and lure them in close to slam them all in one hit, and take out your adversary while he's stunned.

With enough damage dealt, the boss will go down, and Miles will be free to leave and pursue his real task.

Mission 16: Like Real Scientists

Location: Upper East Side

Rewards: 5,500 XP

Warning - once you start this mission, you will not be able to back out and explore Manhattan and get more tokens to upgrade your gear until after completing the campaign.

Defeat the Underground Outside the Science Center

Once you arrive at your destination, take a good look at the abandoned science center. There's two separate boardwalks going around to the main building with Underground on each side - plus two Snipers along the high platforms on each side, and a third sniper at the top of the main building with a friend.

Make the snipers your first priority, and run along the long white platforms to bypass the others until you reach the top sniper first. Use a silent takedown on the sniper's ally first, as they won't notice while aiming around.

Next, head back and take out the two snipers on the side, making sure none of the other Underground on the low building rooftops see you move in. If you're concerned about getting spotted, use your camo or distract anyone nearby before webbing up the snipers onto the high vantage points above.

After them, look for any Underground on the low rooftops along the boardwalk and zip kick into them, using camo if you think another may spot you in the act.

As you begin to take out more of the Underground along the boardwalk, reinforcements may appear by the main building if they start to suspect you, so you may want to periodically check with your scanner for new enemies that may be jumping around to higher vantage points. If they do, follow them with camo to take them out of the picture.

Disable the Generators

Much like the movie theater, you'll find an electrified barrier at the top of the science center preventing access. You'll need to disable nearby generators hidden in the shacks to proceed, but things aren't that straightforward.

Starting with the two closest generators to the building, you can find them in locked shacks, but the gates to reach and disable them are unpowered.

Luckily, the giant sculpture in the center of the water can be spun around, so look so that

you are facing the sculpture and pull the leftmost ball with a node on it towards you, and then again - moving counter-clockwise twice. This should put a node close enough to let you tether to the red nodes on each of the two shacks close to you, unlocking them and letting you drain the generator.

Now, keep the sculpture as it is, and move east to another set of shacks. Only one has a generator on this side, but it's not in line of sight of the ball above. Instead, attach a web from the ball to the left shack, and then daisy chain it to the right shack to reach the generator.

Finally, head to the west side to locate the final generator, and clear out some boxes to reveal the hidden node on the side of the wall you can tether to the last ball.

Now you can return to the de-electrified barrier and Venom Smash through, leading you into the science center proper.

Find Phin

There's a lot to inspect as you make your way through the old science center, starting with the giant screen. To advance, head left into the Virtual Gallery, and note an Underground Cache in the hall on the left side you can swipe for a free Tech Token.

Once you reach the space exhibit, hop down and look for the door to the Sea Living area, and you'll take a walk down memory lane. As mentioned before, there's a lot to see and interact with - including most exhibits you'll pass. Look for the red and white dots to interact with stuff in the Deep Sea area, and then move onward.

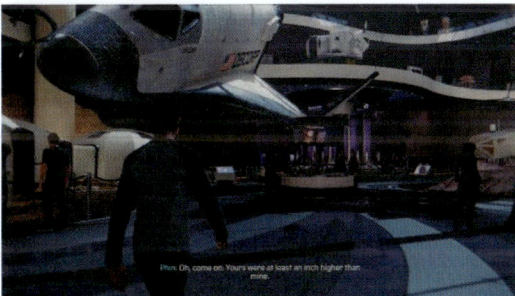

Once in the Space Exhibit, you can check out all the crazy tech on display, including stuff like a memory metal prototype and much more. When you're done looking around, talk to the woman at the elevator only to find that you're going to need to get in through other means.

There's a locked door to the left of the elevator, and Phin will recommend you find a way to slide a reflective surface under the floor that can change shape.

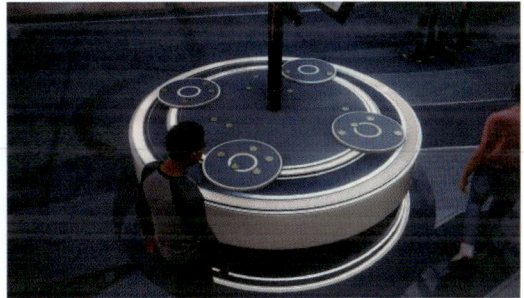

As luck would have it, you can find both things among the exhibits - solar panels near the locked door, and the memory metal back where you first entered under the big space shuttle.

When you interact with the memory metal, you'll need to use your phone to change its shape, so cycle through the different patterns until you find the flat one, and quickly grab it. You can stick around as you leave the memory metal exhibit to get some interesting dialogue from a familiar face, otherwise head back to the locked door.

Once the memory metal is on the other side, cycle through the shapes to find what looks like an igloo - a rounded half circle with a small flat side. Rotate this shape until the solar panel is facing the lock and use your flashlight to light it up.

There's even more things to check out at the Special Exhibit, but your project lies at the far end of the room. Go check it out, and after the scene ends, you'll be back in the present.

Defeat the Underground

Once things start to get crazy, you'll be up against an Underground Brute and his cohorts.

Remember to use the Venom Punch on the shield first, but then switch to Venom Dashes to catch him in his faster two-handed attack style, or he may just dodge the venom Punches or Jumps.

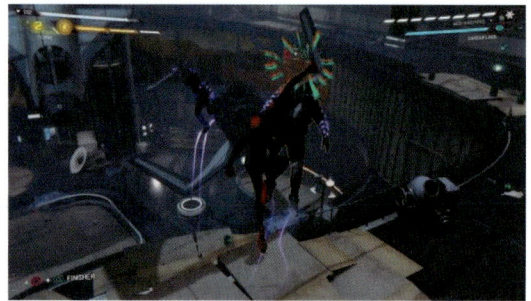

Clear out the first room, and snipers from the space exhibit hall will open fire, prompting you to move the fight into the next room. Keep the guessing by moving up and down the levels to rush the ranged fighters, saving your Venom Punches and Dashes for when the gauntlet and sword-wielders start to show up.

Eventually, a lower level wall will break down heralding the arrival of yet another Brute. Watch out for the firearms flanking his arrival, and lead him away from the hall to isolate and take him down without his friends shooting at you.

38

Move back into the main entrance where you first landed to take out the remaining Underground, and then leave through the hole you first entered to finish this mission and begin the final showdown.

Mission 17: The Battle for Harlem

Location: Harlem

Rewards: 6,000 XP

Stop the War in Harlem

Hurry over from the Science Center as fast as you can, as the battle has already begun, just as a blizzard has hit Manhattan. Be sure to spend any last skill points you can - particularly things like the extra Venom generation, as you're going to need to take down enemies fast and hard.

You'll first find Roxxon and the Underground fighting at C.J. Park, but expect to make your way through a gauntlet of different attackers, fighting both you and their rivals. If visibility becomes a problem, use your minimap or press R3 to highlight enemies nearby.

As you move through the end of the park, be ready for a Roxxon guy with a rocket launcher to show up and try and run interference - throw his missiles right back at him to shut him down. The fight will then spill onto the streets leading to your apartment, with attackers coming in from every which way at the intersection.

This is where you'll want to be using Venom attacks whenever possible to crash into groups of opponents and send them flying, and try to build up your combo meter while watching to dodge incoming fire. Be wary for any Roxxon Shield users who may come running in, and ground slam or disarm their shield first before continuing your Venom assault.

As you clear out the streets, a laser sight will alert you that the fighting has moved to the rooftops, so quickly zip up to engage the snipers and other attackers among the different roofs in the area. There are four rooftops in all here that have assorted forces firing on you, so be ready to zip between them to deal with snipers and disarm them if possible.

Continue fighting along the rooftops heading east until you reach your apartment, where the fighting is the thickest. Eliminate the rooftop attackers before dropping down to fend off two Underground Brutes and two APC with a firing cannon you'll need to yank down. Clear the path with your venom powers and then pick off any stragglers until the street is clear.

Defeat the Tinkerer

When the final battle begins, you'll have to contend with a foe armed with all of the Underground's tech. This means the Tinkerer can swap between gauntlets, a shield, and a sword for a variety of movesets.

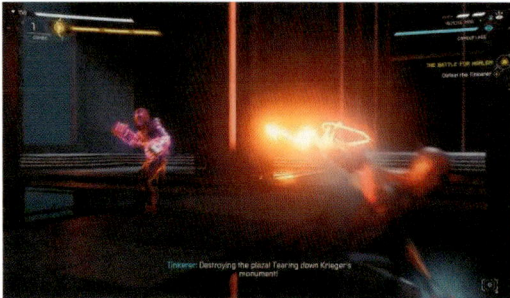

When using gauntlets, the Tinkerer may try to dash forward at random intervals to bait you into dodging before unleashing a powerful blow, so be ready for the spidey sense indicator to know when to get out of the way, and use your Venom Punch to shatter them. If you're low on venom, try and bait out a punch and dodge under her to hit her from behind a few times.

However, she can quickly swap to a sword and deliver long range thrusts and sweeps, as well as an overhand slam that can deal a lot of damage - and will dodge any Venom Punches. If you see a wide purple ring appear, quickly jump up and swing away or you'll be caught in a large shockwave slam attack. The sword attacks are quick, but a perfect dodge can slow things down long enough for you to counter with a Venom Dash and throw the Tinkerer against the wall to stun her.

Don't bother trying to use camouflage to get a jump on the Tinkerer - she'll just toss out a handful of grenades in succession that will be difficult to escape from. Instead, focus on using Venom to disrupt her and press the attack while she's stunned, then be ready to dodge her incoming salvo.

When the reactor starts to pulse, the Tinkerer will start employing new tactics. She can dash far back from you to instantly pull out a rocket launcher and start charging a blast. Counter this with a well timed dash and zip attack follow up, but if you take too long she may jump into the air to employ the large shockwave attack.

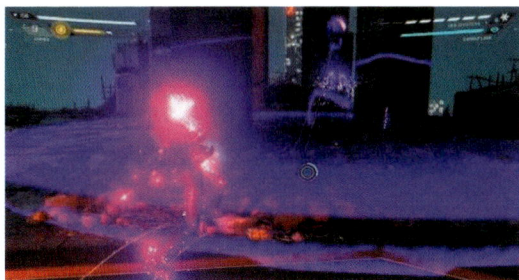

Sometimes if you press the attack too hard, she may counter with a shield to shove you back before sending bolas at you. This can actually work to your favor, as she'll wind up a heavy sword swing down at you - but if you mash square you can escape from the bolas and dodge away - and she'll be vulnerable when her sword gets stuck in the ground.

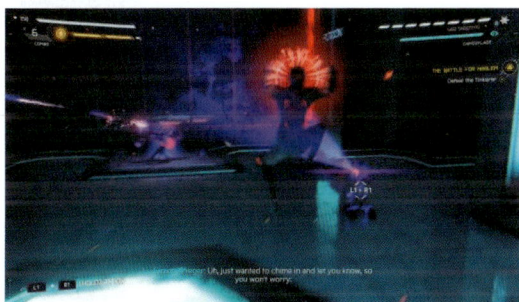

Deal enough damage in this phase, and the Tinkerer will take things to a level below, and unleash even more new tricks at you. After shooting rockets at you, don't lose sight of her - as she'll hop around and place a sentry gun to hammer, throw mines on the ground to erupt in several places, and then unleash a tracking salvo of missiles.

You'll need to quickly yank the turret at her and dodge any incoming missiles or risk getting hit by the burning craters they leave behind.

She'll continue to do this every chance she gets, including trying to knock you back with a shield and bola you in place while she runs to place more turrets and mines. Advance carefully and look for your opening - then don't give her time to retreat by using Venom Dash to hunt her down.

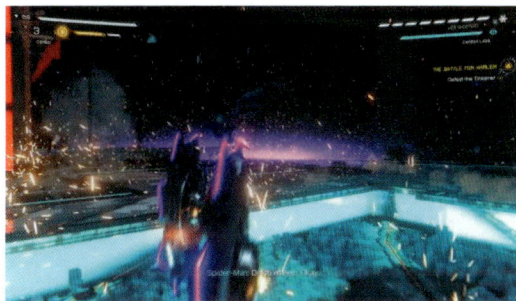

After another cutscene plays, you'll be in the final phase. This time she'll start employing the "Death Wheels", sending rows of saw blades at you that you'll need to immediately dodge. She may follow these up with a bola, but she'll also revert to trying to follow up with a sword attack that you can bait out to get it stuck in the ground.

Be ready for her to rapidly change weapons, from sweeping sword strikes to a homing missile salvo or blades of death, you'll need to be ready for each as you get close enough while building up your Venom Meter to dash into her and cut her attacks short. Just be sure to get only a few hits in, as attacking too many times will trigger her shield bash that can still hurt.

When she starts tossing you to the other side of the room, you're almost there. Dodge the waves of spinning blades, and wait for a triangle indicator to appear to zip into her while she's weakened, and unleash a final assault to bring her down.

With the fight over, and the Nuform reactor going critical, there's only one thing left to do. Make your way to the critical mass and disable it as only Miles Morales can.

After the cutscenes conclude, the campaign will be over. Congratulations, Spider-Man: You've saved Harlem. At this point, there are a few new side missions that will become available, and you can finish up any other activities, or take on New Game Plus mode to unlock a few new skills and even a suit.

Side Missions

Looters

Location: Harlem

Rewards: 1,500 XP, 10x Activity Tokens

Talk to Teo

From your apartment in Harlem, head across the street to the yellow signs for a bodega on the street corner. Inside you'll find the place has been ransacked - but more importantly, a special cat was stolen! Teo will mention the thugs may have moved onto a nearby power station not far from the Roxxon Plaza.

Enter the Power Station and Defeat the Thugs

Head to the top of the large brick building with the four towers past the East Harlem Line, and look for a ceiling window along the roof you can drop into.

Once inside, Zip to the wall and crawl along the left side past some gates to find a way in. In the next room, you'll find a group of thugs, several of which are trying to destroy the transformers. Look below you as you crawl in to find one enemy near a laptop you can web up without anyone noticing.

There are 5 more guys in the room, several with guns, so if you want to try things quietly, head above the one shooting in the bottom right corner and nab him when his friend moves left, then web him up too when he goes up the small stairs. Next, move up along the lights to get the guy firing on the left, and finally crash into the remaining two thugs to take them out fast.

After you're done here, Ganke will suggest you restore power through a backup unit, which happens to be a flickering orange panel with a red light against the wall. Use a Venom Punch to restore power.

Follow Teo's Cat

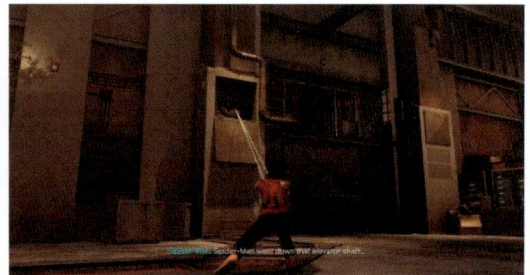

Before anything else happens, Teo's cat will dart off and leave you behind. Use R1+L1 to turn the nearby wheel where the cat was to raise an elevator, and then use R1 to web it in place while you crawl in and give chase. Descend down the shaft and into a grate to continue pursuit into another big room full of enemies.

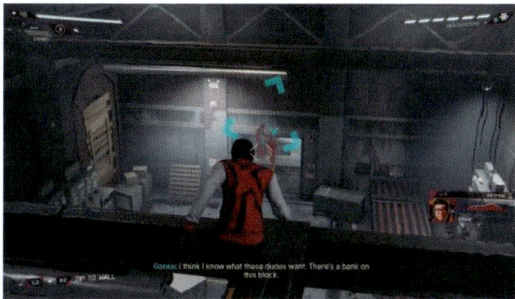

Again, you can try your hand at stealth if you want, but the close grouping means you'll need to distract the enemies with a well placed web shot, then try picking off the guys near the far end first by the stairs, then the patrollers, and finally the ones working on the pipes. Another may notice and run in from the nearby door, so be ready to slam debris in their face to end the fight.

After this group goes down, the lights will go off, prompting you to head down the hall and into a vent leading to another room where 6 more thugs are working.

Only a few have guns, but they also have melee weapons, so take care when deciding who to take down silently and when to go in loud and punchy. Once they're taken out, look again for a nearby backup generator on the wall you can Venom Punch to get things running.

When you're done here, zip into a wall vent leading to the room with the main breaker. There's more enemies here than the other rooms, but there's also room to experiment. Start with webbing up the guy on the second floor, and then turn your attention to the area in front of the breaker. There's a large shelf near the stairs that can be pulled down, as well as two big ceiling fans below your perch point. Just make sure to lure enemies in range either in combat or with some discreet webbing.

Power Up the Breaker

After dealing with the enemies in the room, you'll find that using the breaker gives no results. Press R3 to see the cable line going up to the second floor, and follow it to find a backup generator you can smash to power up.

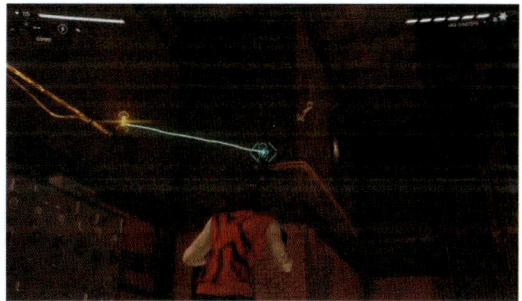

However, the wiring doesn't go all the way along the wall, and you can spot a small gap between two red lights. Aim your web shooters at each of the lights to conduct electricity along your webbing to fully power up the breaker. Before you can finish things up, a brute will come in with Teo's cat, and a bunch of other thugs will come into assist.

Start by webbing up the armed enemies as soon as you can, and spare a few web shots to gum up the brute and leave him disabled while you take out his friends. Use your Venom Punch whenever possible to stun groups of enemies if they get close, and throw debris like fire extinguishers to give yourself some cover.

Once it's down to you and the brute, remember that regular attacks won't do much to them - soften them up first with a Venom Punch, or even a perfect dodge to distract them and then lay into them as hard as you can while he's vulnerable.

More Brutes will come in from above - and it's worth remembering that if you get them on the ground or near a wall, a full salvo of webbing can wrap them and put them out of the fight.

Return to Teo

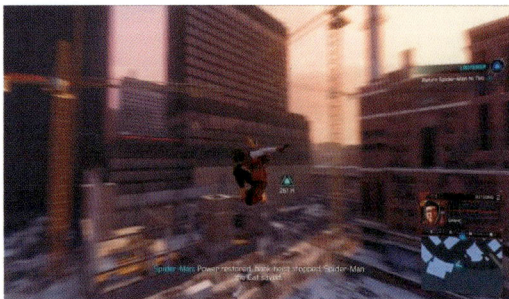

With all the thugs defeated, rescue the cat and flip the breaker, then zip through an open grate to leave the power station behind. Luckily, Spider-Man the cat will hang on tight as you swing on back to the bodega and complete the mission.

Harlem FEAST Shutdown

Location: Harlem

Rewards: 1,500 XP, 10x Activity Tokens

Talk to Gloria at F.E.A.S.T.

Near your apartment in Harlem, head over to the roof of the nearby F.E.A.S.T. Center to switch back to regular ol' Miles and find Gloria outside the center working the soup kitchen. It seems people aren't being allowed back in the center - and Gloria will want you to check on the people nearby.

Enter the nearby park and talk to the couple trying to erect a tent to learn more. After learning some suspicious intel, talk to another couple by a burning can to get more clues. Finally, talk to another group setting up some boxes in the center of the park to find about some suspicious people casing the center before it was mysteriously shut down.

Investigate the Pipes

Head back to the main building and find a door to change back into your Spider suit. Once one the roof, use R3 to scan the pipes leading from the water tower, down around the building and off to the north.

Follow them all the way to the water's edge to find a storm drain that's clogged with debris, and empty it by yanking off the grate.

Since the water still isn't running, your next task is to find the pump station. Scan again to find more pipes moving off to the west along the waterfront before moving south. Oddly enough, it leads to a group of thugs messing with the pump station.

There's a few armed enemies, as well as a brute - and depending on your current gear you might be able to set a few remote mine traps. Otherwise, dive in and stealth attack the Brute first before webbing up and disarming the ranged fighters.

Fix the Three Valves

Once the group is defeated, interact with the pump - but the pressure is off. This means you'll have to find and fix three nearby valves, so get moving!

The first valve is behind a giant trash bin against a wall - yank it forward out of the way, and then interact to seal it.

The next one is located on a low rooftop, and has an old pressure meter - so just turning the valve won't be enough. Once you do, the pipe will burst, and you'll be tasked with sealing the pipe up with webbing, but wait for a moment. The instructions may be unclear, but you'll want to wait for the ruptured pipe to ease the pressure - watch as the red line moves down on the meter to the right. Ready your web shots, and fire when you see it reach the green line in the middle to make a clean job of it.

The final valve is being guarded by a number of thugs, mostly with melee weapons. Smash into them from above if you can, and use the plentiful debris to throw into their faces, and web them up when they fall against the walls. More will appear in a car, so be ready to bash them with their own car doors and beat them down. When the group is dealt with, turn the last valve and head back.

Turn on the Pump Machine

Returning to the site of the pump machine, more thugs have set up shop - complete with snipers on the rooftops, who don't appear to be taking any chances. Zip into the first sniper on the left, and then distract the two snipers below before using camo to take them out one at a time quietly. Take out the last sniper to the left further down.

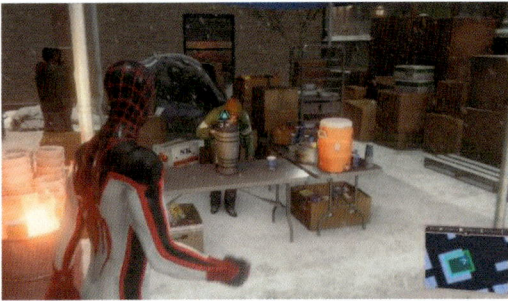

Once they're out of the picture, you can mop up the guys on the ground level until they've all been taken care of, and finally restore flowing water to the F.E.A.S.T. Shelter. Return back and talk with Gloria to update her on the situation and you'll complete this side mission.

Robbers Target Local Biz

Location: Harlem

Rewards: 1,500 XP, 10x Activity Tokens

Talk to Caleb

Head down the street from your apartment around the corner to a hair salon to learn about a string of robberies in the neighborhood. The man will point you in the direction of a shipping center to learn where the missing inventory has gone.

Travel south down to Midtown to search for one of the business owners, only find out they've been kidnapped. Enable your camouflage and drop down to sneak around the cops and inspect a fallen wallet near some police tape and a cart.

Be sure to swing back up to the light posts above to let your camo recharge, then head into the parking lot area nearby where a cop is looking at a discarded jacket. You can try shooting some webbing by the car to distract the cop and the inspect the jacket when he moves away.

Stop the Kidnappers Car

With all the clues gathered, leave the crime scene behind and swing down towards Chinatown - but the police will spook the kidnappers into taking off with Camila in the trunk.

Give chase, being careful to watch your spidey sense for incoming gunfire. Keep pace with the car until you're prompted to zip onto the car, and dodge to the side any thug sticks his head out to pull them out one at a time. Be ready after you pull the driver out to quickly mash square to stop the runaway car, and then bust Camila out of the trunk to learn what the thugs' plans were.

Head to the Docks to Find the Missing Inventory

With new coordinates to go off of, travel further southwest near the FDR Bridge at the Financial District to find out where the thugs have been keeping their stolen inventory. There are many thugs here - but the more

important thing is finding where the supplies are stashed. Use R3 to find important conversations marked by gold, and use your camo to walk past them and listen in.

Luckily, you'll find that your camo meter won't drop during a guard convo, so move between the different groups to eavesdrop, and zip back up to higher ledges if you need to recharge. Keep moving further back among the dockyard east until you find an isolated group of two on top of a crate discussing the stolen supplies.

Now that you know where to look, you can start taking out the thugs one by one. Utilize your camo and distract pairs so they don't see what you do to their friends, and also be aware of all the scaffolding you can pull down, and electrical areas you can zap with Remote Mines if you have them.

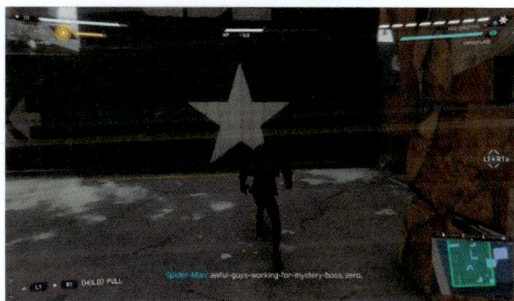

Once the group is taken out of commission, look for the green container with the white star. It's located in the middle of the yard, under one "InterOcean" container, and next to another.

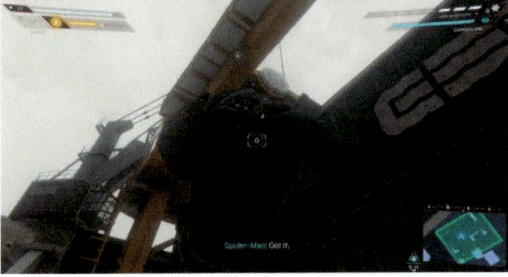

Look up above to find a shipping magnet controlled by a gear, and yank the gear to send the adjacent crate up, and web the gear in place to keep it that way.

Before you can open it up, a handful more thugs will come in via several cars - and some of them are equipped with rocket launchers. You can throw the rockets right back in their face if you time it right - otherwise zip up into their face and unleash a Venom Punch to send them flying, and make use of the many shipping containers as surfaces to web up thugs in.

Finally, head back to the shipping container to get the missing supplies, and you'll complete the side mission.

We've got a Lead

Location: Harlem

Rewards: 1,500 XP, 10x Activity Tokens, Winter Suit

Meet with Hailey

From your apartment, head west until you reach C.J. Walker Park, and look for the girl by the central big stone sphere. She'll inform you that the thugs she tracked were at a shipping center by the river, so travel south along the Upper East Side until you find the shipping area overlooking The Raft.

Defeat the Criminals

When you reach the shipping area, you'll find the place absolutely crawling with thugs of all types - including many snipers posted in vantage points, along with rocket launcher users. It'll be tricky to take out most of them via stealth, but it will certainly help in the long run.

Start by looking for isolated snipers and rocket launchers down by the water, and avoid the sniper beams up above - as they're surrounded by friends. Remember you can lure the guys on the shipping containers closer to vantage points with a well placed web shot.

Once you have a few of the isolated ones taken out, return to the highest vantage point where a sniper and three others are located, and try sending a remote mine to the fuse box on the ground between them. Right as you electrocute the trio, web up the sniper before he can call out what's happening.

The sniper on the containers in the middle will still be a problem, as are some rocket launcher users patrolling around - but you may be able to grab one unaware as he walks around a catwalk.

Once you've gotten as many as you can through stealth, it's time to make some noise - and there's plenty of scaffolding and crates of boxes to tear down and even a crane to bash into some heads to help you. Make sure any other snipers or rocket launcher users that have survived thus far are taken out first, and then concern yourself with the other thugs on the ground level.

When you've cleared out the crew outside the building, look along the ground floor for a shutter behind an old car with a gear you can pull to raise the shutter, then web it in place. Inside, you can inspect a lot of footprints seemingly ending at a tool workbench. Turn around and you'll find a yellow electrical box to open, and it will activate a secret elevator down to a lower level.

Shut Down the Criminals' Comms

Enter the door that appears when the lift reaches the bottom, and note the huge amount of cash on the desk, the rows of weapons, a list of neighborhoods to buy out, and several photos of you. Finally, check out the computer, and you'll finally meet the leader of this gang.

You'll get an ominous warning from the leader, but the connection will be severed. All's well that ends well, right?

Return to C.J. Walker Park and Stop the Attack

Predictably, some people have a problem with you interfering, and you'll need to deal with thugs who are trying to attack innocent civilians at the park Hailey was at. Launch into the thugs from on high with some instant KO zips, and dish out a few holograms to keep the thugs busy while you zip between them dishing out Venom Strikes.

It won't be long before more trucks show up with Brutes, followed by even more cars full of rocket launcher-toting thugs, so be ready to adapt, and use Venom Dash to get across the park quickly to deal with new threats, or disarm long range attackers to shut them down.

When you've finally cleared out the park, the revelers will return, and Hailey will give you an extra special reward for saving the day - a new addition to your spider suit!

Final Test

Location: Greenwich

Rewards: 1,000 XP, Miles Morales 2020 Suit

Prepare for a Serious Fight

Right out of the gate, you'll be fighting a familiar foe from the first Spider-Man game. The good news is that he'll have all the same aerial moves. This mean you'll need to dodge incoming green waves he shoots at you, and get ready for his huge charging swoop attack, then pivot and zip to him to start beating this holo boss to a pulp.

When the boss starts to unleash a string of homing missile attacks, dodge them and look for a prompt to toss them straight back. Do this enough, and you can stun him to zip on over to smack him around again.

As the fight continues (and the story gets weirder), you'll be up against two of the same boss at the same time. This means you'll need to be very careful about staying airborne and ready to dodge at a moment's notice - so utilize the double zip to keep afloat whenever possible, and never land for more than a few seconds.

Note that you can also use your Venom Powers while airborne to score a few more choice hits to keep one of them stunned. Try and focus on one of them at a time so that you'll have less to worry about faster.

When the second boss goes down, your challenge will be complete, and you'll earn a brand new suit - the Miles Morales 2020 Suit!

Back to the Beginning

Location: Harlem

Rewards: Purple Reign Suit

This mission is less of a mission and more of a way to unlock a new suit. It will only appear once you have found all of the Sound Samples in the game after Aaron Davis bids you to find them all.

The last tape will lead you to a hideout under the Harlem Train Station. Here you will find a lot of memorabilia and things you can interact with, but the most important part is the suit left for you - the Purple Reign suit!

Matter Up

Location: Financial District Rewards: Programmable Matter Suit

This mission is less of a mission and more of a way to unlock a new suit. It will only appear once you have cleared all Enemy Bases, which include Underground Hideouts discovered during the Underground Undercover mission, and all Roxxon Labs discovered during the Corporate Espionage mission.

You'll get word soon after of one last hiding spot where The Tinkerer has left a prototype suit. Head to the top of the building, and claim the Programmable Matter suit for your own!

Memory Lane

Location: Harlem Rewards: 1,500 XP, new collectibles

This mission is less of a mission and more of a way to unlock a new group of collections to gather. It will only appear once you've completed the main story campaign.

Head back home to Harlem and enter your apartment using the backpack at the top. Once inside, you'll be able to view Miles' fully converted room, and take a nap on the bed.

Waking up, you'll find a postcard, which will start a scavenger hunt of sorts to find more Postcards hidden through the city - with the first one pointing you towards the museum on the Upper West Side. Find all of them to view a special cutscene!

Cat's Pajamas

Location: Harlem Rewards: Bodega Cat Suit

This mission is less of a mission and more of a way to unlock a new suit. It will only appear once you have completed the main story campaign, as well as the Side Mission Looters that introduces you to Spider-Man the Cat.

Return to Teo's Bodega after the credits roll, and pet the cat in the store. You'll be awarded with a special suit - the Bodega Cat Suit - which lets Spider-Man the Cat team up with you to swing around, and even help perform takedowns!

Essential Spider-Man Miles Morales Tips and Tricks

In Marvel's Spider-Man: Miles Moreals for PS4 and PS5, you'll find really quickly that there's a lot to explore in Manhattan, and a lot of crime to fight.

Whether this is your first time web slinging or you're continuing the Spider saga, we've got some essential tips for both basic hero work, and making the most of Miles Morales' new moves.

Basic Spider-Tips

These tips might be familiar to fans of the previous game, but they're worth keeping in mind while playing as Miles all the same.

Roof Hopping

Most of your time in Manhattan will be spent web-slinging from building to building - and as you get used to the controls, you'll want to maximize your speed and traversal.

Remember that when jumping past rooftops, Zip to Point and Point Launch are better when there's no buildings above you to swing from - and can let you cross roofs quickly in places like Greenwich or Hell's Kitchen. Always look ahead when moving to spot the next point you can zip to, and use Web Zip to gain that extra forward boost to the next rooftop.

When in downtown areas with bigger buildings, you'll find that pressing the jump button after a full swing lets you gain more height, momentum, and a bit of focus for your meter. You can also skim fairly fast across the streets by holding the swing button near the ground and tapping jump to gain small boosts forward at the same time.

You can also perform trick stunts while falling - these grant additional small XP boosts and restore your Venom power in-between fights, making them worthwhile.

Fight In The Air

Aerial Combat is literally the best thing you can do. If you can keep enemies in the air, most of their friends can't touch you - and you can still dodge anyone who can. Make sure to take on combat challenges to unlock the Air Marshall skill early on and increase your damage output and focus generation in the air.

Prioritize Air Launch, Swing Kick, and Air Yank so you can deal more damage and gain more focus in the air without getting attacked, and zip to far away opponents if needed. Aerial attacks can also set you up to knock enemies off rooftops - as Swing Kicks deal knockbacks, and you can press the jump button during aerial attacks to bounce off them and send them flying.

Once you fight enemies who can yank you out of the air, your priority should be taking them out first - this is the best times to use Web Throws or Perfect Dodges to stay grounded but alert.

How to Get More Activity Tokens

Each type of Crime can have up to two sub-objectives for more tokens, and they will be the same when that same type of crime reappears elsewhere in the city.

Any sub-objectives not completed will carry over - meaning you can earn 1-3 per tokens per crime, though once a sub-objective is completed, it cannot be redone the next time that crime type appears, and you'll only earn the base token for stopping the crime.

For more tokens, make sure to use the Friendly Neighborhood Spider-Man App to take on quick tasks or longer side missions to earn plentiful amounts of tokens, and hunt down other side objectives like Sound Samples, Enemy Bases, and more.

The Difference in Web Throws

A lot of combat will probably involve Web Throws, and it's important to note that they behave differently on ground or in the air.

Ground web throws have a slower wind up swing that can leave you vulnerable unless you have the Hazard Zone Skill. Once you have Hazard Zone and even Spin Cycle - you can keep enemies from getting close if you can get through the initial wind up without getting hit - but you may have to dodge and lose your projectile in the process if you don't time things right.

Aerial web throws have a fast wind-up that slams down, but doesn't hit people during the wind-up, and you can't be punched while doing so. You can even chain together several aerial web throws before falling back to the ground, letting you choose when the ideal time to fall back to the ground is.

Although Spin Cycle won't affect aerial web throws, the Collateral Damage skill can!

Don't have time to fully grab an object and swing it before you get hit? It may still be worth doing - once you press L1 + R1, the object will slide in your direction in preparation for the throw, but if you were to suddenly dodge and release your hold - the momentum of the object can still slam in a straight line into anyone in its path!

Wrapping up the Competition

Even more important than throwing enemies is webbing them up. Webbed enemies will stick to almost any surface, as long as you give them a push in the right direction. Three shots from the Web Shooter will make basic enemies sticky, and enough extra shots, or swing kick into a wall, car, or non-destructible surface will stick them permanently. Since Miles doesn't have gadgets like the Impact Shot or Web Bomb, you'll need to rely on his basic web shots all the more to quickly neutralize large groups.

In a pinch, even the Web Throw can do the trick on an already webbed enemy, and this can even work on Brutes and other tough enemies with the proper skills - saving you from an otherwise deadly battle.

Stealth - Quiet vs Loud

Most times you encounter a stealth situation, they will largely be optional - but taking out enemies silently lets you reduce their numbers before the inevitable engagement.

There are two types of sneak attacks - square for close up and silent takedowns that enemies can't detect unless they have line of sight, and triangle for zip takedowns that are louder, but still work if other enemies are far enough away.

Square takedowns are better when isolating one enemy from a friend nearby - but if you an spot several isolated enemies, you can quickly web strike between targets to instantly knock them out - just be sure to ping them with AR targeting to see if it says "Danger" or not to know if they will alert anyone else.

As for silent takedowns, they can be done in many ways - behind targets, under them on ledges, or above them on perches - though a perch can usually only hold one thug, so utilize web shots on the environment to lure enemies to perches that are free.

Miles Morales Ability Tips

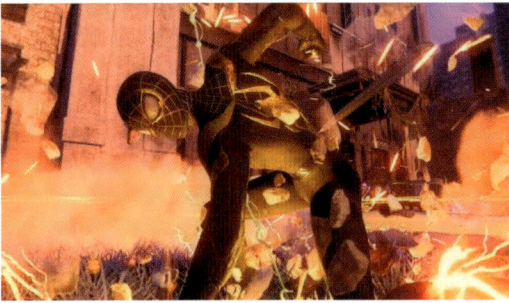

These tips include features and abilities that only Miles possesses, and are new to the series.

- ➢ Suit Powers are no longer tied to a specific suit, meaning you can now mix and match abilities - up to 2 suit and visor mods each. As you unlock more, look for ones that compliment each other, like increasing reaction times for Perfect Dodge AND increasing your damage after performing one.

- ➢ Miles' venom power may seem like a big last resort attack, but in reality you should be using it as much as possible - as soon as you fill a bar even. It's power not just against a single target but the ability to stun nearby enemies cannot be overstated, and is Miles' best bet for shutting down large groups of enemies.

- ➢ Miles may only have 4 gadget types, but one you can build yourself, the Gravity Well, can take spread out enemies and cluster them together. Combine this with Venom Attacks like the Slam or Jump to hit them all in one big powerful attack.

- ➢ Camouflage is an interesting ability that allows you to cloak at will, but uses are a bit more specific than that. Generally, you'll still only be able to take out a single enemy in one hit before others notice what's going on, but you can also use it to get away from dicey situations where you're surrounded. Try using it to get away and heal, or zip over to snipers who may be trying to keep you pinned down. You don't always have to use it to reset an encounter.

- ➢ Not all skills need to be unlocked by leveling up. As soon as you can, try out the challenges Peter left behind to unlock some free skills, as Air Marshall and Payback are some of the best skills you can get.

List of Spider-Man Suits

There are 19 total suits to unlock in Spider-Man: Miles Morales. Below you'll find a list and images of all suits in Marvel's Spider-Man: Miles Morales, along with how to find them, and the skills they unlock.

Many suits can be crafted a few missions into the Main Story, and many more will be unlocked as Spider-Man increases in level. Some suits can only be unlocked by meeting certain requirements or unlocking secrets.

Many of these Suits will also unlock a Suit Mod - a passive bonus that can be applied independently of which suit you're using. Once unlocked, *the Suit pr Visor Mod can be used with any suit you already have unlocked.*

To craft suits, you'll need a combination of different Tokens found by completing various tasks around the city:

Activity Tokens - stopping crime, finding time capsules, completing side missions and activities and more over the city wherever they crop up. Complete sub-objectives in crimes for each type of crime to earn bonus tokens.

Technology Tokens - finding the hidden Underground Caches all over the city, as well as uncovering them in enemy bases.

Sportswear Suit

Suit Mod Unlock: N/A
Unlock Requirements: Default Costume

Spider-Man's default suit that he begins the game with, and has some serious budget vibes. It features a hoodie with a blue puffer jacket, as well as fingerless gloves and athletic pants.

Given this is the first suit you start out with, it doesn't come with any special powers.

Great Responsibility Suit

Suit Mod Unlock: N/A
Unlock Requirements: Complete Mission - Parting Gift

A hand-me-down spider suit from Peter Parker to Miles Morales, this ill-fitting suit is reminiscent of Spider-Man's original classic suit before he made his advanced suit with the white trimmings.

The suit's name is a reference to that famous Ben Parker line - "With great power, comes great responsibility."

Homemade Suit

Suit Mod Unlock: Power Pitcher
Unlock Requirements: Reach Level 5, 8 Activity Tokens, 1 Tech Part

As its name implies, the Homemade Suit is a very DIY spider suit, even moreso than the Sportswear Suit, featuring an all black mask with goggles and a hastily designed logo over a sweater.

It's suit mod allows you to deal more damage with thrown objects, which can really boost your damage output, especially early on in the game.

T.R.A.C.K. Suit

Visor Mod Unlock: Untrackable
Unlock Requirements: Reach Level 6, 10 Activity Tokens, 1 Tech Part

The T.R.A.C.K. Suit, also known as the Time Response Activated Circuit Kinetic Suit, is a unique looking design by comic book artist Javier Garrón. It's almost an inverse of the classic look, replacing the mostly black color with white.

It's visor mod will reduce incoming damage from ranged attacks, which is the perfect defensive tool while you're still getting used to dodging firearms.

Animated Suit

Suit Mod Unlock: Stronger Webs
Unlock Requirements: Reach Level 7, 20 Activity Tokens, 1 Tech Part

Similar to the Animated Suit in the first Spider-Man, this suit also has as stylish cel-shaded look based on many of Miles designs from various comic books and shows. Not to be confused with the Into the Spider-verse suit, it moves at regular speed.

The suit mod, Stronger Webs, gives you more time to temporarily stun groups of fighters and keep them from surrounding or attacking you, which can be very important for giving yourself room to breathe in a big brawl.

Brooklyn Visions Academy Suit

Suit Mod Unlock: Trick Master
Unlock Requirements: Reach Level 8, 12 Activity Tokens, 1 Tech Part

The Brooklyn Visions Academy Suit is a modification to Miles' Classic Suit, throwing on a school jacket and backpack over his existing suit - for those days where crimes won't stop even when you're late for class.

The suit mod, Trick Master, allows you to gain Venom at an even faster rate by performing air tricks while falling. Not as great for combat, but great to swap to between missions or crimes when you have multiple Venom bars to fill.

Crimson Cowl Suit

Visor Mod Unlock: Ghost Strike
Unlock Requirements: Reach Level 9, 14 Activity Tokens, 2 Tech Parts

The Crimson Cowl is a fully red suit with a hood, and partially inspired by its namesake, the super hero Crimson Cowl (aka Justine Hammer who first appeared in Thunderbolts.

The mod Ghost Strike, will allow you to rapidly perform web strike takedowns at range without alerting nearby enemies, rather than having to get close and use slower takedowns.

S.T.R.I.K.E. Suit

Visor Mod Unlock: Venom Overclock
Unlock Requirements: Reach Level 10, 16 Activity Tokens, 2 Tech Points

This Suit is an interpretation of Miles as an agent of S.T.R.I.K.E., the United Kingdom's counterpart to the United State's S.H.I.E.L.D. It features a more armored apperance with powered gauntlets.

The Venom Overclock mod is best used when things are looking grim, as it will increase Venom Power regeneration when your health is dropping. Against tough bosses or encounters, getting Venom back faster can make all the difference.

The End Suit

Suit Mod Unlock: Steady Focus
Unlock Requirements: Reach Level 11, 16 Activity Tokens, 2 Tech Parts

The End Suit is a rugged urban minimal look with camo pants and an open hooded sweater.

The suit mod, Steady Focus, will slow the rate that Camo drains if you aren't moving. In

stealth situations, it can be useful when taking your time to scope out a situation and wait for someone to move - opening up your chance to strike while hidden.

Miles Morales 2099 Suit

Suit Mod Unlock: Venom Suppression Resistance
Unlock Requirements: Reach Level 12, 14 Activity Tokens, 3 Tech Parts

Based on the Spider-Man 2099 comic series, this suit features a sleek future spider design on the front with a small hood and glowing blue-white eyes.

The mod unlocked is a great defensive tools when fighting Roxxon troops. As they throw their suppression grenades and attacks that limits your ability to use Venom Attacks, this mod can lessen that effect, and allow you to use camo to instantly cure yourself.

Into the Spider-Verse Suit

Suit Mod Unlock: Vibe the Verse, Bam! Pow! Wham!
Unlock Requirements: Reach Level 13, 18 Activity Tokens, 4 Tech Parts

Made to resemble the uniform Miles wore in the animated movie: Spider-Man: Into the Spider-verse, complete with the spray-painted design and curious cel-shaded flat looks.

The suit and visor mods that are unlocked through this suit are cosmetic only, and allows Miles to move and act like a comic book character in the specific motion design of the movie - lowering his framerate to be more pronounced against the rest of the world. Attacking enemies will also unleash cosmetic fight noises in true comic book fashion.

Classic Suit

Suit Mod Unlock: Zap Slap
Unlock Requirements: Unlocked after completing mission Time to Rally

This suit is Miles' most iconic black and red design, setting him apart from Peter Parker as the Spider-Man protector of Harlem and its people.

The suit mod is best suited for fighting Underground thugs, as it creates a larger shockwave force when breaking their weapons either in melee or by grabbing and throwing them.

Uptown Pride Suit

Suit Mod Unlock: N/A
Unlock Requirements: Complete all FNSM App Activities

By completing all the small activities given to you around Manhattan, the people will show their appreciation by giving you a modded Classic Suit with a gold trim instead of a red one.

Winter Suit

Suit Mod Unlock: N/A
Unlock Requirements: Complete Side Mission We've Got a Lead

Another variation of the Classic Suit, this suit sports extra accessories given to Miles by his friend, which include a hat, ear, arm, and leg warmers with a striped design. It also features a scarf that will move around as you swing and fight.

Miles Morales 2020 Suit

Suit Mod Unlock: N/A
Unlock Requirements: Complete all Spider-Training Challenges, and the Final Test side mission

By completing every hologram challenge Peter Parker leaves for you, Miles can unlock a futuristic design featuring a helmet with a Daft Punk-like LED display and audio jack headphones built in, as well as an LED chest pattern.

Programmable Matter Suit

Suit Mod Unlock: N/A
Unlock Requirements: Complete all Underground Hideouts and Roxxon Labs, and the Matter Up Side Mission

After taking out all of the Roxxon Lab challenges and Underground Hideout challenges, you'll be clued in to complete a quick mission that turns Miles' suit into a shifting matter suit - using the same technology used by The Tinkerer. It even features special takedowns using extendable legs much like the Iron Spider outfit.

Purple Reign Suit

Suit Mod Unlock: Reclaimer
Unlock Requirements: Complete all Sound Samples and the Back to the Beginning Side Mission

After finding all of Aaron Davis' Sound Samples across Manhattan, complete the quick side mission to unlock a Prowler-esque take on the Spider Suit, complete with the purple and green color style, and even little green claws on the tips of Spider-Man's fingers.

Bodega Cat Suit

Suit Mod Unlock: N/A
Unlock Requirements: Complete the Main Story, and The Cat's Pajama's Side Mission

After beating the game, make sure you have completed the quest where you meet Spider-Man the cat for the first time, and you'll be asked to return to take the cat out for a spin with this suit. It's essentially a mod of the Homemade Suit featuring a backpack where Spider-Man the Cat can hang out in, popping in and out as he pleases. In combat, he may also show up during certain takedowns to scratch at opponents.

Spider-Training Suit

Suit Mod Unlock: N/A
Unlock Requirements: Start New Game+, 20 Activity Tokens, 1 Tech Part

This suit only becomes available to buy in a New Game+ version of the game, so you'll need to beat the game first, after which you can access this simple suit featuring Peter Parker's college t-shirt that he's lent to Miles.

Collections

Like the first Spider-Man for PS4 game, Miles Morales includes a wealth of different collectibles and tasks to do around the city. These range from basic scavenger hunts to challenges and secrets.

Below you'll find a quick overview of all the different types of activities needed to 100% the game.

District	Spider Training	FNSM	Time Cap	Undergrnd Cache	Side Mission	Sound Sample	Hideout / Lab	Postcards
Harlem	1	1	1	3	7	1	0	1
Upper West Side	1	1	1	3	0	1	1	1
Central Park	1	0	1	2	0	1	0	0
Upper East Side	1	1	2	5	0	1	1	1
Hell's Kitchen	1	1	2	4	1	0	1	0
Midtown	1	1	3	5	0	1	0	1
Greenwich	1	0	1	4	1	1	1	1
Chinatown	1	2	2	4	0	1	1	1
Financial District	1	3	2	5	0	1	1	1

Activity and Collections Overview

- **Spider-Training** are special challenges Peter has set for you after completing the mission New Thwip, utilizing hologram technology to test your skills in the areas of Combat, Traversal, and Stealth. There are three sets of each challenge, and completing them will earn you a new free skill, as well as Activity Tokens - more if you earn higher scores. Completing all of them will unlock a special side mission with a new suit.

- **Friendly Neighborhood Spider-Man (FNSM) App Activities** are essentially mini-side missions that have Miles helping people all over the city after completing the mission Time to Rally. These range from tracking down pigeons, finding lost cats, and other small but fun tasks. Completing them will earn you Activity Points, and finishing all of them will unlock a special suit.

- **Time Capsules** are collectibles that appear across the city after completing the mission Reconnecting. Like the backpacks of the previous game, many of these are hiding in plain sight, and only require small interactions to claim them. Each will net you an Activity Point, and some insight into Miles' past.

- **Underground Caches** are special hidden chests available after starting the mission Harlem Trains Out of Service, and will award you with Tech Points for finding them. When near a hidden cache, you can ping it on your radar to close in on their locations. Most are hidden just out of sight, usually involving basic puzzle solving or breaking apart walls or debris to find them. Some of them can only be found in Enemy Bases, and may require a bit of searching before leaving these challenges.

- **Side Missions** are special story-based quests, mostly centering around Harlem and the people within it. Taking them on will earn you extra experience and Activity Tokens, but some may only become available if you've done others first, or beaten the main story.

- **Roxxon Labs and Underground Hideouts** are respective enemy bases, the first appearing after the mission Corporate Espionage, and the second during the mission Underground Undercover. Like the Fisk and Demon bases from the first game, these contained areas are full of enemies you can take on with stealth or combat, and will award you with both Activity and Tech Tokens, provided you find the hidden caches. You can also be awarded additional tokens for completing sub-objectives, and replay them at any time to get them.

- **Sound Samples** are a type of audio collectible that appear after the mission Breaking Through the Noise. These hidden beats are scattered around the city, and will task you with trying to replicate the audio sample by finding the source of the distinct noise and recording it at the correct distance. Finding them will earn you Activity Tokens, and claiming them all will unlock a new suit.

- **Postcards** are a special scavenger hunt collectible that only appears after completing the main story campaign and starting the new side mission Memory Lane. You'll be given clues to track down one postcard at a time, and gain Activity Tokens for doing so.

Sound Samples

Sound Samples are a type of collectible activity in Spider-Man: Miles Morales. Unlocked during the mission Breaking Through the Noise, Miles can then find hidden audio beats from the city itself.

To find **Sound Samples** left behind by Aaron Davis, interact with the green audio waveform hologram, and listen to the noise being produced. You must then zoom in to look around and try and find what is making the noise hinted at in the sound sample. Once you have found the thing that matches the same volume and tempo, reach the required distance from it and record the sound to complete the puzzle.

By completing all of the **Sound Samples** in Manhattan, you can unlock a special Spider-Man Suit - Purple Reign.

Below is a list of locations and solutions for all **Sound Samples**.

Hell's Kitchen Sound Sample

This sound sample is provided during the main mission, Breaking Through the Noise, and is required to unlock all other Sound Sample locations in the city.

The sound sample source is coming from a distant red buoy, just to the north of the site behind a large shipping container. To get to a close enough distance, zip onto the container and record the sample.

Harlem Sound Sample

The Harlem sound sample is located along a diagonal main street not far to the west from the west harlem train tracks.

The sound sample source is coming from the trains themselves - but as they are constantly coming and going, you'll need to be patient and aim your microphone at the tracks until a train passes to record it.

Upper West Side Sound Sample

The Upper West Side sound sample is located in a large alley next to a fire house at the edge of central park, where several firefighters have gathered.

The sound sample source is coming from one of the fire trucks - but you'll need to look around to find the right one. It's located inside the garage itself, the only open garage door past the group of fire fighters.

Central Park Sound Sample

The central park sound sample is located at a frozen lake on the southern side of the park.

The sound sample source is coming from a flock of pigeons that will always come and crowd around a patch of the frozen lake. However, they will scatter if you get close, and won't be able to record an accurate sample. To get the recording, use your camouflage to sneak up on the pigeons and record while they are unaware of your presence.

Upper East Side Sound Sample

The Upper East Side sound sample is located among several high rise buildings in a courtyard with several Christmas decorations.

The sound sample source isn't a temporary festive decoration - it's something more permanent. Head up to the rooftops to spy a water tower that continually drips water onto the roof below, and record the water dripping to find the correct source.

Midtown Sound Sample

The Midtown sound sample is located at the site of Times Square where the major roads converge in the middle of the district.

The sound sample comes from a small unassuming recruiting booth near the south side of the square - look for the brightly lit neon American flag and record the humming of the lights to get the sample.

Greenwich Sound Sample

The Greenwich sound sample can be found at large Y intersection along the streets, just to the northeast of the large Greenwich park.

The sound sample comes from a church not far from the ledge you initiate the sample - just across the street in fact. Aim up at the steeple to record the bells.

Chinatown Sound Sample

The Chinatown sound sample is located in the southeast part of the district not far from an open plaza.

The sound sample comes from very small wooden wind chimes blowing under a traditional red Chinese archway across from your location, with a stairway behind it.

Financial District Sound Sample

The Financial District sound sample is found at the very southern tip of the district along the waterfront, looking off towards the Statue of Liberty.

The sound sample comes not from anything around you, but from the distant ferries sailing around the waters near the Statue of Liberty.

Postcard Locations

Postcard Locations are a type of collectible activity in Spider-Man: Miles Morales. Unlocked only after beating the Main Story Campaign, you can unlock these collectible types across the city by undertaking the new mission back at your apartment called Memory Lane.

After waking up from a nap, Miles will find a postcard with a scavenger note hunt left by his mother. What follows is a series of clues leading you from one postcard to another by finding the locations given on each of the postcard.

Each postcard you find will come with a message, and a clue to the next postcard location - you can only get them in a specific order. Finding them all will unlock a special cutscene.

Below is a list of locations and solutions for all Postcards.

Upper West Side Postcard

Rewards: 100 XP, 5 Activity Tokens

The Upper West Side Postcard is unlocked by getting the first postcard at your apartment in Harlem. The clue points to the Natural History Museum:

"Facing the park, with the world on your shoulders, we guard the next clue."

Find the Natural History Museum on the edge of Central Park on the middle east side of the district. Follow the clue's direction and face the park, and look right from the museum down to the street corner where you can find a sculpture of several men holding up a giant globe. The postcard can be found alongside them next to the man at the back.

Midtown Postcard

Rewards: 100 XP, 5 Activity Tokens

The Midtown Postcard is unlocked by getting the second postcard at the Natural History Museum. The clue points to the Empire State Building in Midtown:

"High atop the empire state, you'll find a pair of blind eyes."

Head downtown to the tall building in this district and run up to the top to find a viewing platform with tall guard rails. Head to the northeast corner of the viewing platform to find a few empty binocular stands - and look for one that has an out of order sign. The postcard will be at the base of the binoculars.

Greenwich Postcard

Rewards: 100 XP, 5 Activity Tokens

The Greenwich Postcard is unlocked by getting the third postcard at the Empire State Building. The clue points to the Museum of Modern Art in Greenwich:

"Find the fossil hiding among the modern. Don't forget to Look Up!"

Travel to the top northwest part of the Greenwich district along the waterfront to find the museum. Looking at the sign on the building, look left for an upper balcony and zip up, and you'll find a large shell fossil on display. Jump on top of the fossil to find where the postcard has been stashed.

Financial District Postcard

Rewards: 100 XP, 5 Activity Tokens

The Financial District Postcard is unlocked by getting the fourth postcard at the Museum of Modern Art. The clue points to the C.O.D.B.s Nightclub and music venue in the Financial District:

"Where money is king, you'll find great tunes, hanging among the lights."

Head down south along the main street until you reach the music venue at the base of a tall building on the street corner. Under the sign for the venue, look to the right of the door for a small stepladder under a single light bulb. If you zip up onto the light, you'll find the postcard on a stereo speaker mounted just to the left.

Chinatown Postcard

Rewards: 100 XP, 5 Activity Tokens

The Chinatown Postcard is unlocked by getting the fifth postcard at the C.O.D.B.s Nightclub. The clue points to a place called Lobster Bills in Chinatown:

"Nestled beneath Stuyvesant lives a monster of a good meal."

Travel to the east side of the district along the rows of + shaped buildings to find the giant lobster and sign at a street corner. The postcard is located on top of the giant lobster itself, on its tail, which you can reach by zipping onto its back.

Upper East Side Postcard

Rewards: 100 XP, 5 Activity Tokens

The Upper Eats Side Postcard is unlocked by getting the sixth postcard at Lobster Bills in Chinatown. The clue points to a place called El Barrio in the Upper East Side:

"No letter enters this artsy castle without stopping at the gate."

Look along the north part of the district for a smaller looking castle-type building among the tall skyscrapers, and head around to the north-facing side of the building. While looking at the sign for El Barrio, notice the large iron gate, and inspect a mail box on the gate front to find the postcard.

Harlem Postcard

Rewards: 100 XP, 5 Activity Tokens

The Harlem Postcard is the final postcard by getting the seventh postcard at El Barrio in the Upper East Side. The clue points back home to C.J. Walker Park, a place just to the east of Miles' apartment:

"Beneath the hoop where you learned to fly, your journey comes to an end"

Travel back to Harlem and enter the park with the large stone sphere sculptures. On the side there are a few basketball courts, look for the the southern court and check around the east hoop for the final present, ending the sequence.

Easter Eggs

Spider-Man First Issue

While Miles' room in his new Harlem apartment changes drastically over the course of the game as he unpacks and sets his room up, you may be able to spot a clever easter egg hiding among his things.

At the start of the game, during La Nochebuena mission, you can look next to his bedside to spot an issue of The Amazing Fantasy featuring Spider-Man's first apperance from Marvel Comics. This is in fact the same cover as the real first issue to reveal Spider-Man as a superhero (Miles could probably sell it for a lot of money!).

Spider Pig!

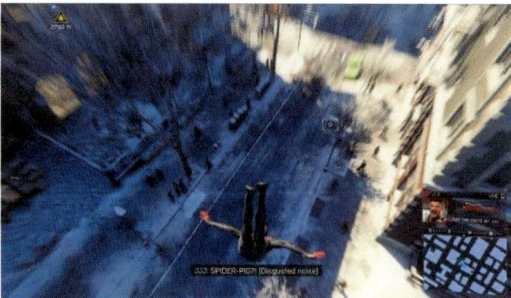

During one of J Jonah Jameson's early podcast breakouts, he'll begin to get angry at the thought of having more than one Spider-Man. When asking what's next, he'll even go so far as to wonder if a Spider Pig is even possible. In fact, it is, as Spider Pig is a real character, and was featured in the animated movie, Into the Spider-verse.

Remembering the Fallen

In the first Spider-Man, you could visit a cemetery in Harlem, where you could pay your respects to Ben Parker's grave.

This feature returns in Miles Morales, as Miles can find the graves of May and Ben Parker side by side, but that's not all.

Not far to the north from their graves is a single site with a group of flowers for Miles' dad, Officer Davis, who was killed in the line of duty. Paying your respects to Miles' father will also earn you a trophy.

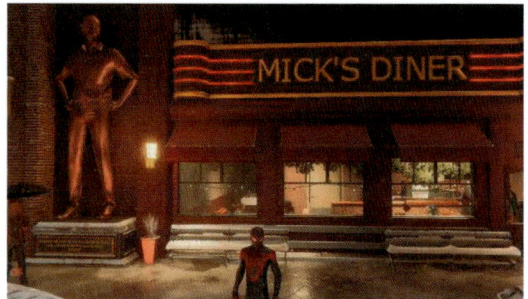

Even real life heroes have gotten a similar treatment. Following his cameo in the first Spider-Man game on the PS4, Stan Lee's appearance has been immortalized in Miles Morales. You can return to the same diner where Peter and MJ bumped into the cameo fry cook, who now has a giant statue outside of the diner in his memory.

Wakanda Forever

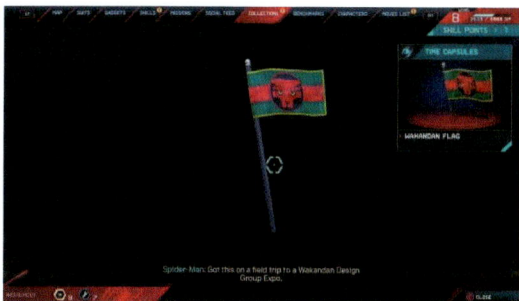

While the previous Spider-Man game made some allusions to Wakanda, home of the Black Panther, so too does Miles Morales. One of the time capsules you can find buried in Manhattan contains a Wakandan flag, and similar flags can be seen during the festival in Harlem.

In addition, the game's credits reveal a memorial for Chadwick Boseman, who portrayed the Black Panther in the Marvel movies.

Vanessa

Wilson Fisk is cold and unforgiving man, but he does have one soft spot. During the mission Underground Undercover, where Miles must infiltrate Fisk's old tower that has been repurposed, you can come across Wilson Fisk's massive vault.

After the battle, look around at the open vaults to spot a rather large portrait of a striking woman. This would be Vanessa, the only person Wilson Fisk has ever cared for. So much so that he's even used her name as a password, which Ganke guesses in a later side mission.

The Mercenaries For Hire

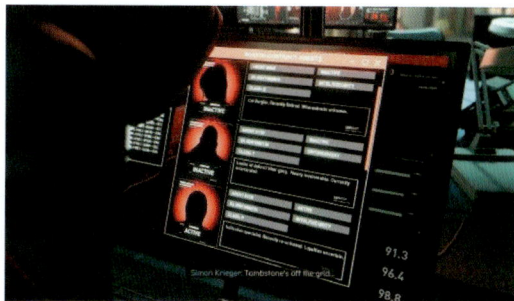

During the mission Tinker Tailor Spider Spy, you'll gain access to several of Roxxon's private terminals to learn more about their plans and the many illegal things they are doing. One terminal at the back of the room has a list of contacts that Simon has considered to use to get some of his jobs, and looking at the screen you can identify each one.

The first for a cat burglar who recently retired is of course Black Cat, who Peter Parker had a run in with during the DLC for the first game. The second leader of a bunker gang is Tombstone, who Peter also tangled with in the first game, and is responsible for his incarceration. The last person... well, you'll find out soon enough.

The Science Center Cameo

You can't exactly miss this one, but it's still worth pointing out. During Miles' flashback of the science center during the later mission Like Real Scientists, you'll have to steal some memory metal. As Miles turns to leave he bumps into Peter Parker, accompanied by none other than Peter's boss Otto Octavius.

Since the flashback is set well before the
events of the first game, neither party has
been properly introduced, but you can stick
around to eavesdrop on them discussing how
memory metal could be utilized in their
current project - which would one would
assume would eventually lead the way for Otto
to create his signature arms.

Printed in Great Britain
by Amazon